112 Miles to the Pin

112 Miles to the Pin

Extreme Golf Around the World

Duncan Lennard

SKYHORSE PUBLISHING

www.skyhorsepublishing.com

Library of Congress Cataloging-in-Publication Data

Lennard, Duncan.
  112 miles to the pin : extreme golf around the world / Duncan Lennard.
      p. cm.
    ISBN 978-1-60239-174-1 (hardcover : alk. paper)
    1. Golf. 2. Extreme sports. I. Title. II. Title: One hundred and twelve miles to the pin. III. Title: Extreme golf around the world.

GV967.L42 2007
796.352—dc22

                                                     2007020216

10 9 8 7 6 5 4 3 2 1

Printed in China

Contents

Introduction

On his first ever round on an eighteen-hole golf course, North Korea's "Dear Leader" Kim Jong-il shot a rather tidy 34. His total, which included five holes-in-one, put him in a commanding position at the top of the Dear Leaderboard at 38 under par. If you have any problems believing this, you can take it up with the seventeen armed bodyguards who witnessed the feat on that fresh October morning in 1994.

Your own introduction to the game may have lacked this burst of spectacular scoring – personally, I managed a mere 20 under par – but I suspect you can remember it vividly all the same. Because, for so many players, golf is a case of love at first smite. I can readily recall the feeling my first properly struck shot gave me; a sensation of fireworks ripping through my soul followed by a warm, spiritual glow that told me I'd stumbled across something special. A glittering tree-lined setting, the sun filtering through the branches, added to the enchantment.

It's the same the world over. For 60 million golfers, the sweetest music they ever heard was the sound of a small white ball ripping through the air for the first time, packed with pace and purpose. That's it; you're hooked. And you are destined to spend the rest of your life trying to rediscover the wondrous feeling that shot gave you.

Sadly, many golfers never do. That first, chance success came at a price; it raised a devil named Expectation. You did it before, so you should be able to do it again. If not, why not?

It gets worse. Once you have established a level of competence with club and ball, golf culture throws you into a world of handicaps and yardage charts, swing techniques and scorecards. The pure joy of that first contact is replaced by an embittered mission to score. If you are not careful, your enjoyment of the game starts to revolve around how well you play.

In a game as difficult as golf, that is not a good thing. The scientists tell us that if your clubface is just one degree off square at impact, the ball will miss its target by seven yards on a 200-yard shot – an astonishingly dispiriting statistic. A three-degree error is enough to send your ball spiralling into the trees.

With the score as the governing criterion, no wonder golf is so often described in terms of pain and suffering. "A five-mile walk punctuated by disappointments" is a common definition of the game. When writer and commentator Jim Bishop claimed, "Golf is played by twenty million mature American men whose wives think they are out having fun," he was not joking. Even golf's patron saint, the celebrated amateur Bobby Jones, darkened the gloomy theme when he famously mused, "On the golf course, a man may be the dogged victim of inexorable fate." How can this be the same game that began with all those early, golden emotions?

This book is about golfers who have realized that golf doesn't have to be this way. The players you will meet do not base their golfing lives on its most frustrating and elusive feature – playing well. Instead, their unorthodox journeys into the game have allowed them to take full advantage of golf's many other qualities – qualities that put them in touch with the reasons we all fell in love with the game.

Take, for example, one of golf's greatest attributes – its setting in the great outdoors. Here we have a terrific opportunity truly to connect with the world around us. But for the score-obsessed wretch, the opportunity is squandered; he's more interested in yardage charts and the navel-gazing that is, apparently, a key part of maintaining concentration.

Thankfully, there are exceptions. A Scot named David Ewen woke up one morning and decided he did not know enough about his home country; he resolved to put that right by hitting a golf ball from the east coast to the west and discovering what lay in between. An American, Andre Tolme, did the same in a country that fascinated him – Mongolia. Their incredible stories, recounted here, reveal golf at last as an outward-looking game, so much at odds with the introspection of the scorecard player.

And what of the field of play? If your mission is to score, you are drawn back to the same track every time. After all, you know it; it gives you your best chance of beating your handicap. Logical, yes: but so dull.

But if your score doesn't matter, you open yourself up to a host of fresh, new experiences. Playing new courses is one thing, but why stop there? Wouldn't you just love to smack a shot over a city from the top of a skyscraper? Or across the field at your local football stadium? Or to the distant shore from a riverboat? This is all in a day's golf for a bunch of Europeans known as Natural Born Golfers, whose aim is to take golf to every place you'd think it wasn't.

In scorecard golf the challenges are stale – a carry off the tee, a high lip in a sand trap, a steep, sloping green. But in taking the game in new directions, the stars of this book have created fresh new problems that sidestep the crushing weight of expectation.

Scientists at Scott Base, Antarctica, must calculate a strategy to stop their precious supply of golf balls being spirited away in the beaks of the aggressive skuas that patrol the skies above. Golfers playing in Greenland's Mount Dundas Open must somehow scale a 75-foot vertical cliff face just to get to the first tee. And after holing out, the nude golfers of New Zealand's Mackenzie Muster golf tournament must develop a way of plucking their golf ball from the hole without giving offence.

And what about the exercise element? Golf is great for keeping you active but it is only the scorecard that limits you to walking. Throw it away and suddenly you have the chance to use the game for your daily aerobic workout. Today, keep-fit golf fans combine running and golfing to form speed golf, a round where you don't so much smell the flowers as hurdle them. Forget Ready Golf – this is ready-steady-go golf.

As for that pure, innocent joy that comes from smashing a ball as hard as you can with complete and utter freedom, welcome to the feisty but uncomplicated world of professional long driving, where the ball flies 400 yards and competitors wear out the grooves in their drivers after just ten shots.

These challenges are fresh and attractive – just like that first shot – and that is why a theme of pleasure and enjoyment flows through these pages. But the journeys in this book are not just about putting the fun back into golf.

USAF Captain George Hall was shot down over Vietnam in 1965. Locked in solitary confinement for eighteen months, Hall kept himself sane by playing a round of golf every day, in his cell, in his head.

A Canadian named Bob MacDermott lost an arm and a leg in a freak accident – but used golf to spur his recovery. Amazingly, he now plays off a scratch handicap. These are stories of courage and survival, a less common journey for golfers to make, but one that reveals the game's true worth.

They are two of the many incredible people in this book. All have forged deep and rewarding relationships with golf through the unconventional paths they have chosen. They have shown me that to look at the game solely in connection with your scoring and ability is to view a vividly colored sport in black and white. No one would dispute the pleasure gleaned from playing a fantastic back nine or watching your handicap tumble; and yet, if we base our enjoyment of the game solely on the numbers we're scribbling on the scorecard, we could find ourselves in for a depressing old time.

These golfers have made me realize just how little I take from a game that has so much to offer, and inspired me to ask for more. I hope they will do the same for you.

1

Scorpions in the Cup

As Apollo 14 shuddered away from the Kennedy Space Center in February 1971 astronaut Alan Shepard – a makeshift 6-iron concealed in his spacesuit – embarked on a secret mission to boldly golf where no man had golfed before. Shepard's lunar course, later nicknamed the Fra Mauro Country Club after the crater Apollo 14 landed by, was approximately 240,000 miles from the nearest pro shop, so it was as well he remembered to bring a supply of balls. Shepard was the same distance away from the nearest pro, so in terms of the technique needed to play a delicate lob over a crater out of moon dust, in one-sixth gravity, he was on his own.

Shepard has no real rivals in his claim for the title of world's most remote golfer. Even the second man to golf in the stars – Russian cosmonaut Mikhail Tyurin hit a shot from the International Space Station in November 2006 – was only around 220 miles from civilization. Tyurin apparently hit something of a shank, which just missed the part of the space station he was supposed to working on. It's golf, Jim, but not as we know it.

Certainly back on earth, most of us do not have to go far to find a track to play. Happily for golfers, the Western world is awash with tees, fairways and greens. In England alone, a slender country that stretches just 400 miles from north to south, there are 2,000 layouts. I can be on the first tee of no fewer than nine of them within half an hour of leaving my front door.

It sounds like a golfer's dream, but maybe this saturation is not all good. Pleasant though these courses are, the experience of playing one is very much like that of playing another. Sure, I can see the sea from one while another has several lakes . . . but the similarities outweigh the differences. I obey the same rules and fall foul of the same hazards; I often play with the same people, indulging in familiar banter and codes of conduct. The experience becomes, shall we say, routine; the courses meld into one.

Of course, a global game like golf is quite capable of offering a much broader range of experiences. But to find them, it's best to get off the beaten track. For it's here, in hidden areas of extreme remoteness, that conformity dies and singularity flies. Convention might be a great colonizer but it is a lousy navigator.

But there is more to the remote golf experience than fresh and unusual sights and sounds. Each club in this chapter is peopled by a singular and sparky membership, golfers whose pure and unbridled passion for the game could teach us a thing or two about our own attitudes to playing. These folks do not care how they play – they are just glad to be playing at all. You simply do not set up a golf course on the ice shelves of Antarctica, or the arid expanses of the Atacama Desert, unless you really, really want to play a game of golf.

But our tour of the world's most remote courses begins in the parched and dusty opal fields of south central Australia. For here, in the middle of a landscape so bleak and lifeless that it is routinely used for post-apocalyptic flicks like *Mad Max II*, there exists a craggy and crusty eighteen-holer.

Opal Fields Golf Club, 400 miles from Port Augusta, the nearest large town, is baked by 104-degree temperatures and is as barren as they come. "In fact, if we see any grass trying to grow we kill it," says club president Kim Kelly. "It gets prickly and bushy and you can't mow it because there are so many rocks around. It's better to spray it."

The course exists to serve the residents of one of the world's weirdest settlements. Coober Pedy is a mining town, thrown up out of the red dust practically overnight in 1915. It turned out the sterile surface was hiding a sparkling secret – the region is home to the world's biggest opal field. Almost a century later the mines are still going strong. Today it is estimated that 95 percent of the world's opals come from Australia, and of those 80 percent come from Coober Pedy.

The intense heat and featureless landscape mean that two-thirds of the town's 3,500 population live underground, in hobbit-like houses called dug-outs. The Aboriginal translation of Coober Pedy is "white man's hole in the ground." In subterranean homes the temperature stays constant throughout the year; even when it reaches 131° F in the height of summer, it's a tolerable 77° F below the surface. And there are other benefits: one happy couple discovered $250,000-worth of gems while tunneling their dug-out. Their home is now more of a warren, with 21 underground rooms.

And yes, in this bizarre, bejeweled mix of holocaust and hypocaust there exists a golf course – and for 66-year-old 19-handicapper Kelly, a government mines compliance officer, it might as well be Augusta National. "It might look like the arse-end of the world round here," he says, displaying the endemic Aussie efficiency in getting to the point, "but we have a lot of fun on the golf course."

The club's 42 members tee off toward fairways that are simply the natural terrain of sandstone and clay rubble, with rocks pushed to either side. "We call them mat-land because if you are in the cleared zone you are allowed to use a synthetic mat to play off," Kelly explains. "Originally the mat was to protect your club. But everyone cottoned on to the fact that if you put the ball right at the back of the mat, it was almost as good as teeing it up. We had to put a stop to that. And then we had to regulate the mats after the cunning members came out with bits of carpet with two-inch-high pile."

Hazards are at a premium. The course has no sand bunkers but a couple of creeks, usually dry, just about come into play. Around the creeks are Eremophila (emu bushes), three or four feet high; elsewhere there are patches of tangly salt bush. Apart from some white out-of-bounds stakes, that's about it.

"Ah, but the fun and games start when you leave the fairway," counters Kelly. "You're in among the rocks. Sometimes you can get a club to it; but more often you can't hit it because of the rock – you'd smash your club. So we have a rock-relief local rule – you can drop away with no penalty. There's an ongoing joke here about some of the blokes carrying rocks in their bag – if they get tangled up in the bush they get it out and claim rock relief."

Kelly is also proud of the greens, which are called scrapes. Inky black, they are made from a mixture of red sand, sump oil and crusherdust – squashed road gravel. Each club member carries a two-foot-long scrape tool. On one side is a rake, which you use to scrape your path to the hole; on the other side is a round pipe that smoothes out your scrape.

"You don't get as much break because they are slower than grass greens," Kelly says. "But you get used to them. When we head off to the cities we struggle on proper greens. The other problem we have is with pitching. The ground your mat is on is sandy, not firm enough to hit down against. You either top the ball or slide underneath it. So we tend to run the ball in with a seven- or eight-iron. And we start putting from 165 feet away."

If all this makes the golfers of Coober Pedy sound serious and competitive, think again. There is a club championship, but most events are fun-based. "We have Eskies out on the course," reveals Kelly, "coolers full of ice and beer. Normally we have two but on special days we'll up it to four. On those days we also have the Booze Bus – normally my Ute – which drives around the course serving water, beer, spirits, port, anything to keep people comfortable. Quite often we get the local police involved. They bring along their breathalysers and give random tests to the golfers. This time they fine people who are *under* the limit."

There are other sights here that add to the surrealism. An eighty-year-old life member named Ralph Underwood zooms around the course on a motorbike, with a sidecar for his clubs. And although there is no dress code as such, South Australia golf clubs are given color schemes. You will see most members playing in green and yellow shirts. But that doesn't stop casual players turning up in thongs when the mercury soars.

And then there is the constant chance of finding a gleaming opal in your divot – although there are no stories of big golfer finds. "You sometimes see potch – colorless opal," adds Kelly. "Also, when we want to patch up a fairway we'll use mull – that's the heap that gets churned up by the mine. You'll see opals in that, bits that have been missed. But so far they've only been worth a few dollars."

Even stranger is the reciprocal deal Kelly has struck with the home of golf – St. Andrews – allowing Coober Pedy members to play for free at St. Andrews and vice versa. Kelly even sent St. Andrews a cheeky letter, congratulating them on getting their course up to scratch. It becomes only slightly saner when you discover that the Links Trust at St. Andrews has been awarded a small opal-mining site, and that the offer only extends to the nine-hole Balgove course at St. Andrews – and only then in winter.

Then there is the climate. The hot months are January and February and most summers will see a four-week run when the temperature never drops below 104°. But according to Kelly, wind is more of a problem. "When it kicks up there is a lot of dust. It's not nice, but it doesn't stop us. The only thing that stops us is rain. If we get rain you have to stop because the earth sticks to the bottom of your boots and you end up ten feet tall. You can't reach your ball."

Kelly understands why people question his sanity for playing such a hot, remote and, frankly, boring course. But he will always emotively defend golf at Coober Pedy.

"OK, the first time you see the place you think, "My God, what a course." But after a couple of games you realize you are going through the same battles any golfer goes through . . . slicing, hooking, three-putting. It's all normal. Here, like anywhere, you can get lost in that challenge; it's a lot of fun.

"But what brings you back to earth is the tourists. We get quite a few coming through, and they go on minibus tours. You look up to see a bunch of Japanese or Europeans laughing at you and taking photos. That's when you realize how stupid you could look, golfing in such a place.

"Yes, golf is different here, but that's what people come for. We get visitors from all over the world and they love it. It looks hostile, but it's relaxing and pleasant. And when everyone else is shivering, it's nice here."

Three thousand or so miles to the south of Kim Kelly and his thong-sporting, sun-basking cronies, another group of golfers are definitely shivering. The lime-green buildings of Scott Base, Antarctica, are home to some eighty scientists. The average temperature here is $-1°$ F, pretty much the same as the freezer in your kitchen. Yet for the small but fanatical group of golfers among the scientists, this is nothing but a nip in the air. To their eyes, a frozen empty continent is no reason to stop swinging.

Golf has been played at Scott Base – at 77 degrees latitude south (Cape Horn is a mere 57 degrees), just 838 miles from the South Pole – since 1961, four years after it was built. As you might guess, the terrain is not exactly a course designer's dream. The "course" is always set up on an impromptu basis, with usually eight (it can be as few as five) holes spread out across the refulgent slopes of Ross Island. That's more out of necessity than choice: Ross Island – a floating ice sheet 500 feet thick and fed by glaciers – has a particularly capricious landscape. It must contend with constant pressure ridges that can turn a level hole into a roller coaster. One year the golfers found the fairway of the third hole, laid out just 24 hours before, now possessed a one-in-four gradient.

Nevertheless there are few courses with such an exotic backdrop. Apart from the walls of snow and ice, the 12,000-foot Mount Erebus – the world's southernmost active volcano – dominates the skyline.

But erupting volcanoes and holes that change shape are nothing compared to the Scott Base golfers' biggest problem – maintaining a reasonable supply of golf balls. For, whether you know it or not, a golf ball is very much the same size and shape as an Adelie penguin egg. Adelie penguin eggs happen to be the preferred diet of Antarctic skuas, large and aggressive gull-like birds that patrol the skies above the base. And while skuas are expert hunters and nest-builders, they are rubbish at telling the difference between a Titleist and a penguin egg.

"Sometimes they won't be able to get the ball in their beaks," says Alastair Pringle, a keen Scott Base golfer in the 1990s. "Instead they will roll the ball to one side or the other and sit by it. So you will find your route to the hole veering off to one side or another. You can hit a straight drive down a straight hole and still end up playing a dogleg."

Indeed, the skuas ensured golf at Scott Base got off to a rather bad start. Several players ventured out on to the sea ice to compete for a silver beer mug, but gave up after their balls – painted red – were swooped on and carried off by the birds. The problem has never really been resolved.

After the shape-shifting holes and the skuas, a third problem even these scientists struggled to solve involved footprints in the snow around the hole. Eventually this was remedied by a new rule – at Scott Base you are deemed to have holed out if your ball is within your body-length of the pin. This of course gives the advantage to the taller player – although the downside is having to prostrate yourself in the slush to stake your claim.

Although Antarctica is about as remote as you can get for a golf course, there is an American scientific base at nearby McMurdo and golf competitions are occasionally played between the two. There is a tradition of awarding unusual prizes for the best individual score. One of the best, put up by the Americans, was an "exotic dancer" – in fact this was a blow-up doll. "Everyone was driving the ball like hell that day," recalls Scott Base golfer Bob Le Master.

Scott Base had its golfing heyday in the eighties and early nineties. In recent times the activity has declined. "In the last few years the golf's been pretty infrequent," says current base manager Mike Mahon. "To be honest I don't even know where the trophies have gone. These days, when an outside game is played it's usually on the sea ice in front of Scott Base. And we tend only to use putters."

There has, however, been an upturn in mini-golf, with some of the winter crew designing and playing a course right through the rooms and corridors of the base. Well, if you were stuck indoors in the dark for six months, what would you do?

Meanwhile, in northern Chile, South America, the problems are not cold and darkness, but aridity. The Atacama Desert is officially the world's driest place. Protected by a Pacific high-pressure system to the west and the Andes to the east, its average yearly rainfall is 0.01cm. Parts of it have not seen rain since records began 400 years ago.

Some place, then, for a golf course. Yet the Atacama is where you'll find the 7,000-yard Club de Golf Rio Lluta. Leonardo Jimeno is one of the club's hundred-strong membership, and he is quick to point out that a round here is very much a case of virtual reality.

"There is no vegetation at all, so we must improvise," he reveals. "We have marked several zones with stones painted blue; these are our lakes. If you hit your ball in there you must take a drop, just like normal golf. The only difference is you can find your ball.

"Then there are areas marked by green stones – our forests. On two holes we have taken dead palm trees from the coast, cut them up and propped them on boards. Fairways are marked with a pair of white chalk lines. Between these lines you can play off a mat. Outside these lines you must play the ball as it lies, which means among the thousands of desert rocks. This is why we have a special local rule allowing a fifteenth club – usually an old iron that you don't mind smacking into the rocks. It saves you damaging your set."

Greens, which are coffee-colored, are made up of seashells, sand and motor oil. One hazard you might think a desert course would have no trouble making authentic is the bunkers. But even then, the local rocky stuff is overlooked in favor of a finer imported variety.

Guests are cordially invited to complete their rounds by midday; most afternoons sandstorms kick up dust devils that swirl across the eighteen-hole layout. They are also warned to look into the hole before retrieving their ball; the cups are a favored retreat for sun-shy scorpions.

It is arguably one of the most remote and hostile environments for golf. But remote golfers have an amazing knack of seeing that as an attraction, and Jimeno has no trouble explaining the pleasure of playing in such a place.

"I compare it to American football," he says. "The ideal might be to play in the Yankee Stadium with the grass and all the lights, but you can play the game anywhere – in the street, in a park. It's the same game. A bad swing gives you the same feelings of frustration whether you are on a perfect strip of fairway or in the Atacama Desert. But those feelings are short-lived; the important thing for all of us here is simply that we have an opportunity to play our favorite sport."

This fundamental pleasure found in being able to play the game they love is common to all remote golfers – and the key to why the game can flourish even in the most barren conditions. It is a pleasure to which we have perhaps become insensible, blessed as we are by the ease with which we can get a game.

It is also revealing to see how the relief of simply being able to play frees golfers from the suffocating clutches of etiquette. I don't know what your club secretary would make of it if you turned up on a steamy Sunday morning in a thong. Similarly, something tells me that letting the senior members scoot round on a motorbike is a long way off at most British clubs. Bellowing at the bird life for the privilege of hitting your next shot would, I'm sure, be classed as ungentlemanly; and if you paused to check the cup at every hole for deadly creatures, you would no doubt get a two-stroke penalty for delaying play. Manners breathe propriety into golf, but they can also suck the life out of it.

The pure pleasure of simply being able to play, and the freedom that goes with it, is something I had not experienced for a very long time. It was time for that to change. With that in mind, I set out to play the United Kingdom's most remote course.

Colonsay is a small but rugged chunk of igneous rock in the Inner Hebrides, a group of islands off Scotland's west coast. Three miles across and seven long, it claims 300 species of wild flower, 123 species of birds and 120 humans. To journey here is to travel in time as well as distance: the island has one pub, one bank and one primary school, attended by just ten children.

It does, though, have a golf course. In fact, it has had one since 1880. Once abandoned, its existence was only rediscovered in the 1970s when the islanders chanced upon a 1920 map detailing the layout of the lost links. They decided to resurrect Colonsay GC, and the course reopened in 1978.

And now, after a night in the island's only hotel, I am in the deserted car park – well, patch of gravel on the side of a one-track road – of this forgotten and faraway track. I push my enveloped $40 through the slot of a decrepit honesty box, instantly becoming a fully paid-up member of Colonsay GC for the year. Colonsay is not only the UK's most remote course, but also its cheapest. I am, however, denied a view of my course. The car park is in a dip, and the only clue to the whereabouts of the first tee is a worn path up the hill; it could easily have been made by sheep.

Instead it has been made by my fellow members – and at the top I am greeted by a truly epic landscape. A huge swathe of grass, daisy-swamped, runs down to semicircular flaxen sands. On the other side of the sand is a cobalt and clamorous Atlantic Ocean, and on the other side of that is Goose Bay, Canada. To either side, black angular hills frame the scene. It is picture-perfect.

There's just one problem – I have no idea where the first hole goes, and there's no one around to tell me. The fairways of Colonsay GC are mowed by 200 or so sheep – but so is the rough. Straining, I spy a red flag 300 yards yonder toward the sea. Some primal golfing instinct takes over and I know it is the first green. No fairways means no rough, so I have about two square miles to aim at. A lay-up would be the equivalent of stitching kneepads on to your pyjamas. I pull out my driver.

Club selection – or lack of it – is one of a hundred things I find myself free of at a place like Colonsay. Never mind yardage charts, I don't even know how long the hole is. There is no slow play and no par, no dress code and no decorum. I could run, jump around, shout my head off if I wanted to. Only a few ewes would care. I could even forget the course layout and hit to any pin that takes my fancy. There's no one around to complain.

But the biggest thing the place frees me of is an obligation to try and shoot a low score. I realize this after my pitch to the second apparently lands on a trampoline, the ball vaulting fifty yards past the green. On closer inspection I find no trampoline. I do, though, spot a lump of granite, bursting up through the small area of mown grass that masquerades as a putting surface.

Sheep crap of indeterminable crustiness is everywhere. I know I will lose balls in the daisies. I am not going to break the course record today, partly for these reasons and partly because no one knows what it is. Released from scorecard hell, I set out to rediscover the guileless glee that comes simply from thrashing a ball with a club.

After six holes of this glorious, mindless and careless golf, I am starting to get the hang of not caring if my putt lips out. On the seventh tee I stop to drink in the scene once more. Just as I decide I am the only human around for miles, I discover that I am not even the only golfer. A mile away in the haze across the sward, in sight but out of hearing, I make out a figure driving from a tee. Within minutes we are shaking hands. His name is Seumas McNeill.

"I suppose I am the club president," he says with a gentle Scots burr, smiling at the extravagant title. "I sort out the summer parties and competitions. Which we don't have very often."

McNeill confirms club membership is "somewhere over a hundred," and tells me he plays once a week. He is a sheep farmer by trade, and it is his sheep that graze the links.

McNeill's wife is club treasurer. "We have agreed that the green-keeping budget for the course is whatever is necessary," he announces. I am impressed, until he adds, "We don't spend anything that isn't absolutely necessary."

Colonsay GC is somewhere between low-maintenance and

no-maintenance. Human influence extends to flags, tee markers and green mowing. Everything else is completely natural – even the bunkers, patches of exposed sandy soil whose random location proves Mother Nature has no concept of risk-reward strategy.

In fact Colonsay's green-keeping requirements pretty much dictate the green fee/membership sub. When the course reopened in 1978, the cost was $2 a round. Despite a brief spell at a fiver, it stayed at that price until 1998, when McNeill broke his mower on one of those mid-green rocks. To cover the cost of a replacement, the five-man committee put the fee up to $20 for a year's membership. It has now risen to $40 to accommodate having to pay the new green-keeper, some new tees and dealing with a rabbit problem. "The sheep sleep on the greens because they are the driest areas," says McNeill. "That's all right. But the rabbits want to dig holes in them.

"But even then, this is a magical place to play golf. You're in among the wild flowers and the rarest birds in Britain. You have the Atlantic for a backdrop. Even in the height of summer you can play a round without seeing another soul. You just don't get held up. It's so good for your stress levels. The view from the first tee alone . . ." There is no need for him to complete the sentence.

I bid Seumas McNeill farewell and complete my round in the same carefree manner I started it. I don't know what I shot, and I don't care. For the first time in years I watched the entire flight of the ball on my tee shots. If music is the space between the notes, then golf must be the walk between the shots. By that rationale Colonsay Golf Club is up there with Pebble Beach or Augusta National. At $40 for a year's play, it might just shade them for value.

Playing at Colonsay reminded me of playing as a kid – no expectations, no worry, just plenty of fun. For the first time in years I did indeed experience the true pleasure of playing – and all I had to do was get off the beaten track. Yet for some golfers, off the beaten track does not necessarily mean remote: a new wave of player is redefining the game by bringing it to an environment that is equally alien but rather closer to home – the city.

BMWs for Bunkers

Traditionally, golf and the urban environment have mixed like nitric acid and glycerol. As long ago as 1887, American golf pioneer Robert Lockhart was hurled into prison for trying out his new clubs in New York's Central Park. He had been reported to the police by a group of old ladies who had been, according to reports, petrified by his aggressive ball-striking. Fortunately for Lockhart, golf was so new to the States at that time that no legislation existed to cover it. There was certainly no law against "Use of the Mashie-niblick in a Built-up Area." Lockhart was released without charge.

However, historians have discovered that the first ever mention of golf in the States – which came in 1659 – related to the banning of street golf in New York's Albany district. Things were not much better in the United Kingdom; urban golf was played in the mid-eighteenth century in the Grassmarket area of Edinburgh, but its perceived danger and nuisance value made it a short-lived venture.

Strangely, it is only in the last fifteen years of golf's 600-year history that urban golf has gained any meaningful momentum – and in recent times the game has exploded. Today there are city golf groups in Belgium, Switzerland, France, Germany, England, Holland and Australia. America has a network of urban-golf communities in San Francisco, Seattle, Chicago, Austin, Boise and Des Moines.

Why the game is suddenly flourishing in this infertile environment is less easy to quantify, but it would appear that an ever-stretching band of golfers is deciding that you don't need space and natural beauty to enjoy a good game of golf. For more answers, we must turn to the people who play the city game with such verve.

It's a shimmering autumn afternoon in Hamburg, Germany. At the weekend the city center is deserted; the only movement is a blue and white boat pulling slowly away from the dock.

The boat chugs into the harbor, and stops. On some unseen signal, raffishly dressed men and women burst from every door, pouring on to decks and bow like a pirate raiding party. But instead of wielding swords and cutlasses, this crew brandishes 8-irons and wedges. And instead of a defenseless merchant ship, they are about to attack an unguarded strip of shore.

For the next hour golf balls – special eco-versions that dissolve in water – rain down on a huge piece of green tarpaulin depicting a skull and crossclubs. The whole scene is played out to a roaring soundtrack of jarring synth and guitar, courtesy of a street punk band on board. Ask for silence on your backswing and expect to find yourself walking the plank.

Welcome to Natural Born Golfers, the punk golf movement busy taking the game to every place you'd think it couldn't be played. Since founding NBG in 1992, German Torsten Schilling has organized games in pretty much every environment you can think of – with the obvious exception of a golf course. A recent escapade saw his mob using the wreckage of a crashed Cessna jet for a target. They habitually hit from rooftops or through deserted inner-city streets; industrial and regeneration areas are other favored venues. They once hired a barge for the day and stood on the roof, firing shots at a target on the riverbank. Another time Schilling, a TV studio designer by trade, built a mock living room on a pontoon, which he launched out into the harbor. The gang spent the next half-hour trying to put a golf ball through the TV screen from a distance of 120 yards.

This is a brand of the game that's become known as Crossgolf, apparently in homage to the ancient French/Belgian game known as *jeu de crosse*, in which a wooden ball is hit across fields. There are no rules and no scoring; fun is the sole objective. And today Schilling and his mates are in the middle of a Crossgolf marathon. It started at 1 p.m. with a rendezvous at a soccer stadium. They hired the Millerntor-Stadion, home ground of Third Division team St. Pauli, for the afternoon, and the players spent the first hour hitting balls up the pitch off two mats.

"Sixty people were supposed to turn up," Torsten had muttered to me. "But it looks like we have about a hundred and fifty. I'm not sure how this is going to work on the boat."

His fears were well founded. Now, as the party hits full swing onboard, the captain of the ship ushers Schilling to one side. "We have a problem," he says. "The depth gauge on the boat is not working. I don't know if we are in twenty meters of water or one meter. It's too dangerous to carry on."

Schilling reluctantly agrees and, after some difficulty, draws the pelting of the green tarpaulin to a halt. Ever resourceful, he simply asks the captain to sail the boat the other way, into known deep water. "The shoreline is full of targets," he shrugs. "We'll find another one." Sure enough, he spies a big container on a dock construction site. So the group shells balls at that.

Punk golf it may be, but Schilling does in fact have permission to do this. "This is one of the amazing things," he crows. "We always seem to be able to get permission. No one minds. Hitting golf balls in crazy places is a lot of fun but we don't want to annoy or hurt anyone."

There is indeed no one around, and the golf proceeds with no raised voices or clenched fists from the land. Most shots plop in the drink – others ping around the docklands. Occasionally, one tonks the container, resulting in a raucous cheer.

So far I've not come close with any of my efforts. The bobbing boat has played hell with my weight shift, and my concentration has deserted me. A low-handicapper like me should be doing better from this range. I look up to see a Dutch guy staring at me and see myself through his eyes; a serious golfer trying too hard, and getting stressed by the failure. In the context of the day and the surroundings, it must look ridiculous. We're on a boat, for goodness" sake. Looking around me, it is obvious that Torsten's clan are not expecting anything from the golf; it is simply a focus for the fun. Their constant laughter and merriment reveal that it's quite possible to have a good time without good golf.

On the way to the next venue, the top of a 165-foot building known as Medienbunker, Schilling admits that Natural Born Golfers – a community that boasts 150,000 people on its mailing list – has been labeled golfing anarchy.

"It really isn't," he insists emotionally. "It's not that we don't like normal golf; it's just that we don't care about it. It doesn't mean anything to us. Every time I saw it on TV it looked so boring. Yet when I first hit a ball it was fun. So I wanted to play some more but I never thought of joining a club. Never. It's just a different world. You see these guys and it's all 'Quiet, please,' 'Don't stand there' . . . and the rules, my God! 'OK, my ball is lying under a leaf, what happens now? What do I do?' And their clothes! It's just a totally different world. Nobody from our community plays on a golf course."

Schilling reckons a typical Crossgolfer is very open-minded and free-spirited, which he claims is "definitely connected to this rock and punk thing. Nearly ninety percent are actors, musicians or work in media. And they are always very nice. Within twenty seconds they are in the group, even if you've never met them before. They are definitely wild. The wildest people I ever met."

No kidding. A hundred of them are now climbing the steps to the roof of the Medienbunker. It so happens that the roof overlooks the stadium of St. Pauli FC, and the next hole sees us flogging balls into the center circle, 110 yards away. It is a fitting target: St. Pauli has become a symbol for punk. Its logo, similar to NBG's, is a skull and crossbones. Its fanbase is overtly political, extolling antiracism, antifascism and antisexism.

By now I have managed to ditch my try-hard attitude. It's freed me up to feel the full excitement of hitting a ball from this genuinely extraordinary tee. Predictably, my success improves as my effort wanes; I hit three foam balls inside the center circle.

Because of the diversity of locations, Schilling has come up with a range of balls devised to fly different distances and which will cause differing degrees of pain to unsuspecting passers-by. In all there are 25, and clever use of rubber, foam and sponge means there is a ball for every occasion. Now we are using a ball with a hard shell like a normal ball but with a reduced weight. It flies three-quarters the distance of a normal ball, perfect for this range of shot. There are biodegradable balls for the water and glow-in-the-dark ones for night games.

"We once played a tournament at a hotel in Berlin, which has two buildings 225 feet apart," Schilling recalls. "So we jumped on the roof of one building and put the target on the other one. But the front of the building was the hotel windows and glass, and over the back was a street that we couldn't close. So we needed a ball that could not fly over the building but could reach the target, yet if short wouldn't break any windows. Our ball range meant we had the perfect missile."

On the way to the stadium he talks about the rise and rise of NBG. It started in 1992 when, bored and bacchic in a hotel, he started fiddling about with some clubs that were needed for a studio set. A course sprung up in his hotel room, then expanded to the hallway, where he experimented with chipping and pitching. "First the ball stuck in the wall; then I crushed the ceiling. We had to fix it before the morning."

Schilling and his mates then got into the habit of playing every Sunday in the harbor. It was not organized; they would just walk around, spy a target and hit toward it. People showed an interest and began to join in. They took to sneaking out in the evening as the city center emptied, playing with glow-in-the-dark balls.

NBG got a big break in 1998 when a journalist from German *FHM* magazine saw a party they were staging after an event and asked what it was all about. He ran a feature on the group. Since then, Schilling reckons media coverage has quadrupled every year. There are NBG offices in Paris, San Francisco, Warsaw and Kuala Lumpur, as well as seven in Germany. An NBG event is also the latest and coolest thing in corporate entertainment: IBM, AmEx, Microsoft, Volkswagen, even a Formula One racing team have asked Schilling to stage days for them.

An NBG tradition is always to play the last hole into a bar. So, using all available doors and windows, the Natural Born Golfers jemmy and coerce their spheres into the clubhouse of the soccer club.

"At this stage we would normally do the golf-cart race," says Schilling matter-of-factly. It turns out NBG has bought some Harley Davidson golf buggies, made in 1969, from the States. When thrashed, they'll do up to 30mph. "They are very cool. We have the only golf carts in Germany with a road licence. I go shopping with them. Sometimes we jump on them at night-time and go off and play through the streets."

But today there is no time and little space, as 700 people are shoehorned into a room designed to take 500. A rock band called Smokeblow, big in Germany, strike up.

Later, it's time for the prize-giving. In keeping with the spirit of NBG, prizes don't go to the best players, or even the best shots. Instead the first of three awards goes to a chap who had never played before but was "sensational and very funny." The second goes to nine Poles who had made the trip from Warsaw. The final and main prize doesn't go to a golfer at all, but to the band that played the street punk on the boat.

The day ends with a live punk karaoke – you don't sing from a computer, you are the lead singer of a band. As the boat band plays Sex Pistols, Ramones and Green Day, golf punks sing, drink and dance. And Torsten Schilling is buried in the middle of them.

Before Torsten Schilling and Natural Born Golfers, urban golf was limited to publicity stunts. In 1969, Open Champion Tony Jacklin revived a tradition started by 1920s American golfers, including Walter Hagen, of trying to carry the Thames from the roof of London's Savoy hotel – a 400-yard carry. He struck it 353 – into the drink.

In 1977 a 48-year-old Arnold Palmer, visiting Paris for the Lancôme Trophy, was still a relative unknown in France. To rectify that, he shinned 300ft to the Eiffel Tower's second stage and shelled a bunch of balls down on the city. From this vantage point his longest hit was measured at 403 yards – though it was his last shot made the headlines, the ball pinging off the street and landing in an open-top bus.

But now, Natural Born Golfers has seen to it that the face of urban golf has had some serious plastic surgery. Schilling can justifiably claim to be at the forefront of this modern craze for taking golf into the city. For since his lead in 1992, urban-golf organizations have been springing up through the tarmac. San Francisco now holds its own urban-golf day. And in France, Le 19me Trou (the 19th hole), a group of just six, play through the streets of Paris.

"We play simply for pleasure, and because it's free," says Bastien Lattanzio. "We can speak, drink beer, smoke cigarettes, listen to music and we can wear what we want. We've tried real golf, but prefer the liberty of this game."

Le 19me Trou play pretty much every day. "We have no competitions as such, but play a range of games," adds Bastien. "In Montmartre we hit into a garbage can 30 feet away. Or if we can, we'll hit balls into the Seine from as far away as possible. At weekends we'll play in building sites or roadworks where nobody is working."

Le 19me trou has even proved a splash with the traditionally reserved Parisians. "The underground like us because they see us as a deomcratization of a rich sport," confides Bastien. "As for the others, they find it funny because it is so paradoxical and new. And they are not worried; we use a safe, soft ball on the street."

But while city golf in Paris is still very much underground, in London it is on its way to becoming a regular, mainstream activity. Every year, the streets of East London are closed down to let golfers play through. This is the Shoreditch Urban Open, first staged in 2004 and gaining in popularity every year.

It is played by 64 contestants over an 18-hole course whose hazards substitute warehouses for woods and BMWs for bunkers. Soft, beanbag-like balls fly a maximum 110 yards, while holes are below-street-level water valves, opened with the permission of the local water board.

For the Shoreditch Urban Open competitor, the challenges are intense and immense. Imagine your backswing is blocked by a motorbike; your path is hindered by a rubbish skip and a wire fence. You ask someone for the location of your target – a fire hydrant – but no one seems to know. The ball you are about to hit is lying in a gutter and as aerodynamic as a sewer rat. You take your stance four inches above the ball, thanks to the kerb, while being goaded by a dozen beery blokes watching from a pub window. And finally, somewhere around the top of your backswing, the last vapors of your concentration evaporate in the glare of a loud and very insistent car horn.

The event came from the fevered imagination of London architect and frustrated golf-club member Jeremy Feakes. "I once had to pick up my clubs and carry them through London," he recalls. "I remember walking through Covent Garden and all the faces looking at me as if I was an alien, just because I had golf clubs on my back. It struck me as quite funny. One guy looked especially strangely so I decided to ask him if he had seen my ball. That really nonplussed him. I think this was the moment a city golf tournament occurred to me."

For Feakes, the tournament had dual attractions. First was the challenge, close to an architect's heart, of routing a course through a cityscape. He lived in the increasingly fashionable Shoreditch district and knew its office blocks and warehouses made for quiet weekends. Even then, it took him nine months to acquire the necessary permissions from the police and Health and Safety. In the meantime he pounded the pavements, looking for a street corner that could form the basis of a fiendish dogleg, or a car park that he could label out-of-bounds yet tempt people to carry.

"I was determined to re-create a full golf course in the city," he says. "I wanted its eighteen holes to present the same level of challenge a green golf course poses. I didn't want pitch and putt."

In 2005 Feakes even managed to route a hole through a graveyard. "It's now a small park. I'm not sure if there are any corpses down there but I know enough time has elapsed for land-usage change."

Feakes' second inspiration was to have a pop at the exclusivity and snobbery he feels exists in traditional golf clubs. He still remembers the rough ride he got as a junior club member, including a time when the lady captain walked out on to the fairway in front of him and started praticing. "When we asked her what she was doing we got the whole 'do you know who I am?' treatment. Next thing I know, I'm getting a letter from the men's club captain asking me to see him for 'a chat.'"

This is why there is a web-based Shoreditch Golf Club with a stack of mock petty rules. There's a lifetime ban for anyone who refuses to let the committee use their mobile phone; there is a fine for shouting "Get in the hole"; and amid a batch of clothing regulations are four instructions for the correct positioning of the peak on your cap.

The event is open to all, and although 350 apply for the 64 spots, selections are made via a questionnaire designed to elicit who is most passionate about playing.

Despite the radical nature of the Shoreditch Urban Open, this is a real golf event with proper strokeplay scoring and no handicaps. The winner has the lowest total. And while most players are aged between 22 and 40, one of the best urban golfers is a teenager named Ollie Clarke. A score of 32 over par might not sound any great shakes, but Ollie's total was good enough to win him the 2005 event – fending off tour pros Ronan Rafferty and Ross McFarlane in the process.

So what's the secret of great city golf? "I'm not sure," shrugs Ollie, whose six-foot-two frame earned him the nickname Iron Giant. "But one thing I noticed early in the round was that a nine-iron hit the leather pouch ball as far as a three-iron or wood, and was much easier to control. So I used short irons when everyone else was trying to slog the cover off the ball."

His tactics bore fruit on one hole where he felt confident enough to cut a 90-degree dogleg round a sandwich shop by taking on the carry over the top. "It was risky but I made it. The ball ended up ten feet away."

Ollie used his head in other ways. He saw that, unlike normal golf, hazards could be used rather than avoided. So instead of threading balls between tower blocks, he thrashed into them, judging the rebounds. He negated the arbitrary nature of putting – the "balls" aren't especially round and show little interest in rolling straight – by using the gutter to hold the line.

But Ollie's enlightened approach could do nothing about the major hazards – cars. "It's a shot penalty if your ball rolls up under one," he reveals. "You can have a go at the ball but you are likely to get fined for causing damage."

Despite Ollie's success with the short irons, his older opponents – perhaps lacking a competitive edge through the event's unofficial "drink, drink and be merry" ethos – failed to catch on. His only moments of anxiety came from a couple of waved fists from nonplussed motorists, outraged to find a barrier and a golfer blocking their path.

"The event is a lot more fun than normal golf," insists Ollie. "There are no rules, no petty etiquette . . . and the variety of shots allows you to play more outlandish shots and to show off a little."

Somehow, the Shoreditch Urban Open manages to pay homage to the game of golf while taking the mickey out of it. Contradictory it may sound, but it's born from the modern golfer's typical view of the game – a thumbs-up at golf but a slightly longer digit raised at golf culture.

"It's a strange mixture of tradition and innovation," admits Feakes. "The Shoreditch Urban Open needn't be punk golf, but that's kind of how it's worked out. I guess we are all making a statement, and that is, 'Golf is great and we can play it anywhere – and if we want to play it here we will.'

"I'm not a club member. I'm strictly public courses, because I like the freedom, the looseness of dress code. It gets away from the outdated dogma that exists in many British golf clubs. There's no reason for it."

Feakes has tournaments set up for Edinburgh and his heart is set on staging an event through the fluid maze of Venice. But above all he is desperate to see plans through for a Cape Town event. "Cape Town golf is completely white," he says. "We'd love to take half from townships and half from the clubs, get them all playing together. There's a lot of inspiration to be had there. It will help us reach our long-term goal – of driving out the rubbish that can be found in the philosophy of golf."

Urban golf is becoming the perfect antidote to the sometimes restrictive nature of the traditional game. The everyman location takes away the exclusivity; the excitement of the unusual shot-making adds freshness and vibrancy to the challenge; and, as I discovered in Germany, the preposterous lies and hazards remove any expectation of competence, which makes the experience a lot more fun. This is golf's freer and lighter alternative, even when it takes the form of "serious" competition. But when it comes to pitting your wits against your fellow golfers, the Shoreditch Urban Open is merely one of many bizarre tournaments held around the planet – and not even nearly the most extraordinary.

3

Dress Code – Socks Only

Regular golf competitions are won and lost on some of the most manicured turf on the planet – shaved, smooth greens, trimmed emerald fairways and pert teeing grounds – often raised to give the duffer the illusion of a soaring drive. Everything, in fact, to help us get round the course in fewer shots.

Logic would have us believe all this preparation is a good thing. Of course, it isn't. Perfect conditions merely rob us of the ability to form a plausible excuse for a bad shot. With no half-credible alibi to call upon, we play the game with hearts made heavy by the weight of insufferable pressure.

That pressure is not eased by the traditional game's insistence that golf courses should be, above all things, fair. Shots should be justly rewarded or punished in perfect ratio to their quality. In this way, a fair course cannot help but reveal the best player. Indeed golf's most famous course, St. Andrews, is routinely lambasted for the illogical and unpredictable bounces caused by its corrugated fairways.

The principle of fairness might be acceptable on the world's professional tours, where people are striving to make a living out of the game and millions of pounds and dollars are at stake. But for the average Joe, the knowledge that he's not going to get away with any miscues only adds to the tension. Not only that; the fair golf course – everything calibrated with clinical, scientific sterility – makes for a dull and predictable round of golf. My guess is that even traditional golfers, while proclaiming the virtues of the great tests of golf, have a secret soft spot for some quirky, crazy little nine-holer where every hole is irrational and therefore engraved into the memory.

Fortunately, the denizens of the outer reaches of Planet Golf realized the downsides of fair, well-maintained courses years ago. They envisaged a carefree, pressure-free world of low expectation and high drama, in which we would have to drive the ball through waist-high mountain savannah, finesse a delicate pitch shot out of a morass, or lag a downhill putt over scree. And so they wasted no time swapping pristine pasture for untameable terrain.

In this heady fusion of exhilaration and futility no one, least of all yourself, expects you to post any kind of a score. And with that weight lifted off your shoulders you can actually settle down and enjoy the game. After all, that's why you're out there.

Diego Solis is miffed. His twelve-foot chip, struck expertly from a thin green mat placed on rocky shale, has just scurried straight into the foot-wide hole, cannoned off a stone in the bottom of the pit and ejected back out again. It's the second time that's happened this round. "Jeez, I'm not gonna win this thing with that sort of luck," he mutters, and a clammy cumulus of condensation covers his nose.

"This thing" is the twentieth Mount Dundas Open, without question one of the strangest golf tournaments in existence. It is played out each July in northwest Greenland, on top of a mountain so precipitous that the competitors must climb an 800-foot slope just to get to the first tee. The final 75 feet of that is vertical cliff face, which the golfers must scale with ropes.

"That climb took me half an hour," sighs Solis. "I was bushed when I got to the top. I didn't like it much either because I'm not great with heights."

On gaining the summit, his mood failed to lighten at the sight of a helicopter landing with a cargo of golf clubs. When he asked for an explanation, he was simply told that it would have been impossible for competitors to carry their own sticks up the hillside climb. Then, even more infuriatingly, he had been issued with just two irons. "They just told us they wanted to increase the difficulty rating," Solis shrugs.

The view from the first tee of this amazing course isn't that much more hospitable than the journey to it. There may be no snow on the top of Mount Dundas in July, but what remains is an aggressive and muscular terrain strewn with rocks and solid, semi-frozen clods of earth. Somewhere out there is a fifteen-hole course, but no flags are visible because of the crazy undulations. "The longest hole is only about a hundred and fifty yards, but I think every tee shot on the course is a blind one," adds Solis. "You arrive on the tee and there's someone waiting for you. He just points vaguely, saying 'There you go, hit it over there'."

The course is also littered with chasms. On several holes you must walk and play along a ten-foot-wide precipice, either side of which are sheer drops. Today's 35 competitors are warned not to get too close to the edge. There is also a ball-preservation rule in force; two over the edge and you must forfeit the hole and move on.

Things don't get much easier at the green, either. A coquettish ring of rocks marks out the "green," luring you toward it only to reject every advance. You must chip the ball over it to find the inner, foot-wide stone circle that represents the hole; a putter here is as useful as a chocolate chainsaw. Not easy, especially when every time you actually manage to hole a shot it bounces out again. But that's the least of Solis's problems.

He's made it to the eleventh, and his thin green mat is giving up the ghost. "You can't get it level because of the rocks underneath," he says. "So for one thing the ball rolls all over the place. As soon as you get it stationary you really need to start swinging. But even then it's fifty-fifty whether the ball moves before impact. But the problem is that because the mat is always uneven I keep taking chunks out of it. We all do. I'll be lucky if it lasts till the fifteenth."

The rocky terrain is making the bounce of the ball completely random – on the rare occasions Solis gets one straight, the ball kicks off at right angles on landing. On one occasion it bounces straight back, almost to his feet.

Then there's the weather. The Mount Dundas Open is always contested in July, but Greenland's version of high summer rarely sees temperatures climb above freezing. Today it's 24.8° F. There is a 30-knot wind, lending the air all the charm of serrated steel. Despite this, Solis is wearing only jeans and a sweater, running between shots to keep warm. At one stage he overdoes it, stripping down to a T-shirt and peeling off his thick, Arctic gloves. After a hold-up in play, they are soon back on again.

Like the Masters, the field for this special event is strictly limited. But we can safely say that's where the similarities with Augusta National end. Competitors are drawn exclusively from personnel at the nearby U.S. airbase at Thule, less than a thousand miles from the North Pole and 700 miles inside the Arctic Circle. Solis is a staff sergeant in the 821st Security Force. Thule, pronounced *too-lee* and meaning "northernmost part of the inhabitable world," is (unsurprisingly) America's northernmost airbase. It is the only U.S. airbase to have no permanently assigned aircraft. It does, however, have a tugboat.

The base forms the backdrop to Solis's final shot of the round. The good news is his mat has just about held out; the bad news is that he's not going to win. He taps in for a commendable 69, against the par of 56, and well adrift of the leaders. Even with all the running his foursome have taken an average of twenty minutes per hole, completing the course in five hours. But there are no penalties for slow play; on the first tee the starter informed his group not to hurry as they had about three-month's worth of daylight left.

Despite all the hardships, it has truly been a round to remember. And besides the lack of expectation and pressure, Diego Solis is quick to grasp one other benefit of extreme-terrain competition. Forget handicapping and its mathematical mazes – a corrugated surface is the only leveller you need.

"I'm not a member of a club," says Solis. "I just play occasionally with buddies. But I heard an announcement for this event and thought it would be an interesting thing to do. And it was. We play for bragging rights. With all the rocks and weird bounces, the game up here is one hundred percent unpredictable. That gives me the chance to put one over on some decent, seasoned players. I may not have won, but at least I managed to do that."

The Mount Dundas Open might not identify the best player, but it is not meant to. The competition embraces the elements of chance and luck, elements that have all but disappeared from modern, traditional golf, but ones that add fun and excitement – as well as reminding you that golf is, after all, a game.

Whether golf courses should be fair or not, one thing that traditionalists and innovative golfers tend to agree on is that the game is best played fully clothed. This is not necessarily the view of the average anti-golfer. For anyone wishing to attack the sport, the subject of our clothing is usually a pretty good place to start. For one thing, we are all apparently fashion-unconscious, craving diamonds, plaid and garish prime colors. Also, we evidently like to look fifty years older than we are, as this seems to be the principal criterion behind the sport's ardent quest for an arcane dress code.

But do not worry. A group of bronzed New Zealanders has come up with the perfect riposte: naked golf. Since 2001 a golf tournament *au naturel* has been a popular and keenly contested part of the MacKenzie Muster naturist festival, staged every summer on New Zealand's South Island. Each year around forty nudists from across the globe take over the local golf course at Lake Tekapo to compete for a beautiful trophy in the form of a wine cask.

"We play an individual Stableford off full handicap," says Kiwi Rod Thrower. "The rules are that you must tee off in the nude and play the last hole in the nude. In between you can put some clothes on if you wish, but that's only to take bad weather into account. Normally it's around the low seventies, so we don't bother."

To the uninitiated naked golf raises a series of questions, not least of which is, where do you keep your tee pegs? "Oh, you have a few options," Thrower explains. "You can wear socks and shoes, and some folks tuck pegs and ball markers into their socks. You could stick a peg behind your ear too, but I just use a compartment in my golf bag. Then there's always your bum, but I would definitely treat that as a last resort."

Thrower is a keen 20-handicapper and club member at Lincoln GC, Christchurch. But according to him the practicalities of naked golf are no different to playing fully clothed. "The game is the same, the scoring is the same. People ask me about etiquette, things like bending over to tee up or getting the ball out of the hole. Maybe on occasion I'll bend at the knees a little more; but to be honest, naturists don't really think about that sort of thing."

There are two other essentials for the nude golfer. "You need a hat and plenty of sun block – all over, you have to," Thrower advises. "We have an ozone problem and we're very conscious of it." Fortunately the stripped swingers have nothing to fear from insect bites: mosquitoes only appear in the evenings, while the sandflies tend to stick to the South Island's west coast.

Thrower decided to play in the event because "a nude golf tournament sounded hilarious." But both he and organizer Kay Hannam are quick to point out that, while being a lot of fun, the event is a lot more than a giggle.

"As a movement we've gained credibility," says Hannam, "even just by using the word naturist instead of nudist. People connotate nude with rude and think that it's a sexual thing. It couldn't be further from the truth. People phone me up and ask if the men get hard ons and so on, but it's just a load of rubbish. There might be the odd person who rises in the sun, I don't know. But that's probably more to do with what's going on in your mind than because you're looking at a lot of bare bodies."

"The tournament is definitely a mixture of fun and seriousness," confirms Thrower. "Some golfers play barefoot, and they tend to be the non-golfers who are just out for a bit of fun. But there are plenty of others who take it seriously because there is a really lovely trophy to take home. Any regular golfer would be keen to win it."

When it comes to promoting golf's ultimate dress code New Zealand is by far the world leader. Away from the Mackenzie Muster tournament there are several naturist resorts with golf courses while a second big nude golf event is held at Nelson. Elsewhere in the world nude golf is barely on the radar, if you'll pardon the expression. There are a couple of small naturist resorts in the States, and one or two in Europe, but very little organized golf.

Despite New Zealand's acceptance of naked golfers Thrower has failed to convince his fourball at Lincoln GC to give golf in the buff a go. "They all say, 'Oh, yeah, that'd be great, I'll do it if you will,' and things like that. I'm not sure if they'll ever make it.

"Playing golf nude is a personal thing, like all naturism. I much prefer playing naked. I can't in all honesty say I play better nude, but there's more freedom. Your swing is not impaired by anything. When I go back to normal golf I find myself constantly thinking, God, I'd much rather play the other way."

"Being nude is holistic," adds Hannam. "It goes with exercise and looking after yourself. It's a basic freedom. You can't express the liberty that you have without the hassle of clothes.

"And if you don't buy that, you can't deny it cuts down on the washing and ironing."

If Rod and Kay have given you food for thought, munch carefully – it might be as well to inspect your club's dress code first. When three young Welshmen – Nick and Peter Kehoe, plus Gareth Rees – popped out for a few holes at Maesteg Golf Club in 2004, clad only in their spikes, they were banned for three months.

The reason given to them for the ban was ungentlemanly behavior, although the sound of cheering from the assembled ladies in the clubhouse suggested that not everyone disapproved.

But if there's one tournament where you might be tempted to give naked golf a shot, it is the aptly named Heatstroke Invitational, an event played in America's hottest place at the hottest time of year.

The tournament takes place every July at Furnace Creek GC in Death Valley, California, a course that can claim the diabolical double of being America's lowest and its hottest. You will strike your first tee shot 200 feet below sea level – and typically in temperatures averaging 113° F. Here's one golf event where you don't want to be setting a blistering pace.

"Don't leave your irons in the sun," advises tournament organizer Matt Utter. "You'll scald your hands pulling them out of the bag." That's why competitors in the Heatstroke Invitational tend to drape towels over the tops of their bags. It's just one of the tricks you'll need to survive this, the steamiest of all golf events.

Utter, a sales director for Silverstone Golf Club in Las Vegas, came up with the idea in 2000 after hearing about the extreme conditions at Furnace Creek. "I asked some of my friends if they were up for a uniquely thermal challenge. About eight came along. Now we have sixteen to twenty."

And Matt's guide to surviving eighteen holes in a cauldron certainly does not include stripping off. "Wear white, turn your collars up, pile on the sun block and drink. And drink. I guess we are guzzling about three litres of water a round. The guys at the club are great, setting up the coolers for us at the start and more at the turn."

Despite the sustained sensation that you are sticking your face into an oven, the Heatstroke Invitational remains competitive. Over the years the golfers have played a variety of formats, from two-person best balls to Texas Scrambles to team events. There is always a nearest-the-pin and longest drive, though the thick sub-sea-level air renders results in the latter less than impressive. "You need a club-and-a-half more because the ball just gets knocked out of the air," Utter reflects.

Mercifully, no competitor has yet suffered heatstroke. Utter cites the biggest problem as fatigue. "Your head just gets kind of cloudy. One year, coming up the last, I was so worn out I could not complete my swing. The ball kept leaking out to the right. It's so hard to focus. Everything is against you. I would say scores are five to ten shots worse than average."

This brutal event appears to confirm the extreme golfer's stop – start relationship with sanity. But for Matt there is nothing odd about it. "The heat is the challenge, the lure," he argues. "Don't you want to know what the hottest round of golf possible on the planet feels like? After all, if you're going to play in Death Valley, you might as well play it when there's a chance you might die."

It's roughly 2,300 miles from the USA's hottest place to one of its coldest. At 3,500 square miles Kodiak is America's second largest island, behind Hawaii only. Thirty miles adrift of the Alaskan mainland and some 250 miles south of Anchorage, its silver peaks rise out of the northernmost reaches of the Pacific Ocean. Kodiak is best known for its vibrant population of the world's largest bears; Kodiaks weigh about the same as a car and grow up to ten feet tall – neither of which stops them being able to run faster than you. But the island is less famous for an equally fearsome sight – a one-hole, snowbound golf course up the side of the 1400-feet Pillar Mountain. And, as the mountain's name suggests, those sides are steep.

The Pillar Mountain Golf Classic is always played out in the last week of March, when temperatures first start to nudge up toward freezing and the bears are, perhaps, starting to think about coming out of hibernation. First staged in 1984, the open-to-all event reached a peak in 1995 when 52 players made a bid for the top and glory. More than twenty years later there is still a steady stream of golfers only too ready to become vertically challenged – though the field has dropped to below twenty.

Like the landscape, the golf is untamed and virtually lawless. "There are only two main rules," says Pillar Mountain golf veteran Micky Mummert-Crawford, "and they are related. First, no chainsaws. There are loads of Alder bushes on the mountain but we can't have everyone running about with chainsaws, clearing a backswing path. You can use a handsaw, though, if you like.

"Second, do not wake the bears. They should still be sleeping at this time of year. It's a five-shot penalty if you wake a bear, although you can convert that into ten strokes off your score if you subsequently manage to evade it."

Each golfer is allowed one caddie and one spotter, the latter playing a vital role as a lost ball carries a two-shot penalty. Canny competitors douse their balls in fluorescent paint, which tends to leave a telltale trickle in the snow. Your ball is played as it lies, but you can dig the snow out around it. Despite this, scores for this one-hole course have been known to range from in the 20s to more than 700.

The event came about more through desperation than a desire for a wild challenge. Kodiak may be big, but it didn't even have a course until 1986, when the nine-hole Bear Valley opened. None of which was any use to two bored fishermen, Glen "The Cod Father" Yngve and Steve "Scrimshaw" Mathieu, who were drowning their sorrows in a local bar one March night in 1984 during the closure of the commercial fishing season. The keen golfers struck a fifty-buck bet that they could hit a golf ball to the top of nearby Pillar Mountain in fewer strokes than the other. Word got around, and the next day seventeen more golfers assembled at the bottom of the hill, waiting to join in the quest. So began the Pillar Mountain Golf Classic.

The route to the top is up an old bear trail. What with the snow, the slopes and the searching, the golf is a sluggish business. Indeed, the event is held over two days. The last push to the top is precarious and especially laborious. "It's steep and it gets icy up there," recalls Mummert-Crawford. "One year we had to take our gloves off because we needed our fingers for the purchase to climb."

And your reward for the exhausting climb to the top? A wobbly green in the form of a circle of lime-green jelly, in the middle of which is the hole – a five-gallon bucket. Perhaps the true reward comes when you hole out and, in that first rush of achievement, look around you – south to an epic panorama of snow-capped peaks and west to the cobalt, crashing Pacific, with any luck embellished by the sight of a whale's plume.

"I guess that feeling is one reason why we put ourselves through this," adds Mummert-Crawford. "We also raise a lot of cash for local charities and scholarships. But I've played in fifteen of the twenty events and what keeps bringing me back is quite simply the satisfaction of being able to say, 'I've done it!'"

Golf-course architect Pete Dye once observed: "The ardent golfer would play Mount Everest if somebody would put a flagstick on top." Perhaps nobody has actually tried that yet, but then none of the estimated 1,500 Everest conquerors had the foresight to take a flagstick with them. But the playing of the Pillar Mountain Golf Classic – and all the competitions in this chapter – reveal Dye's remark could yet prove to be a case of true words spoken in jest.

The Pillar Mountain Golf Classic might be one of golf's more outlandish events, but in one respect it is as traditional as the Open Championship itself: the winner is the player with the lowest score. What a yawn. OK, it's a scoring system that tends to reveal the best player . . . but that hardly plays to the strengths of the vast majority of the world's players. Imagine a scoring system that did not vaunt birdies and eagles but instead celebrated mishits and oddities – things that, after all, we are quite good at?

In fact, you don't have to imagine it, because there is a tournament that does just that. It is called the Trashmasters, a charity event held every year in Aspen, Colorado. The tournament's organizers have come up with a unique scoring system designed to take the pressure off trying to play well – and to reward interesting shots, as opposed to good ones.

You will, for example, earn two points for a "Willie" – a shot that bounces off a buggy path, named after Willie Nelson in honor of his song "On the Road Again." A "Seve" – any escape from rough longer than six inches – will gain you a point, as will a "Skippie" – a shot that skims the water but ends up playable. To earn a "Barkie" (and a point) your ball must hit the trunk of a tree. But a "Tin Cup" – in which you manage to keep your score in single figures despite three visits to the water – will net you three points.

In all there are 24 such ways to score. "Trash golf encourages a free-spirited golfer and definitely rewards the risk-taker," says event founder Boone Schweitzer. "The scoring favors the player who likes to cut the corner or go for an improbable carry. Those types bring the Trashmasters scoring system more into play."

The Trashmasters has become a glitzy event, with celebrities including Michael Douglas and Robert Wagner taking part. But entry is strictly first come, first served. Even the likes of Jack Nicholson have fallen foul of this rule.

If you win you'll be awarded the coveted Golden Jacket, which – like the green one awarded to the winner of the Masters tournament – is guaranteed to fit.

The Trashmasters format could come across as a bit of a gimmick, but a closer look reveals it is anything but. The Trashmasters, in fact, does nothing less than redefine golf – and in a rather profound way.

My dictionary defines golf as "a game in which the object is to hit a ball into a series of (usually) 18 holes in as few shots as possible" – and of course, that's what we all try to do. But you really should try playing a round in which the "in as few shots as possible" part is relaxed. Golf becomes a very different game. So many new dimensions are added.

When my three-ball tried it, we awarded points for brave shots and deducted points for safe ones; good heckling won marks, as did the ability to withstand it; arrow-straight shots were marked down; you had to draw or fade your way down the hole; tee shots gained marks for finding fairway bunkers; and putts gained marks for lipping out. It may not have been golf as we know it but it was relaxing and creative, feisty and fun . . . and it probably improved our skills too.

Naturally, the challenge of trying to score is one of golf's biggest draws – and it will always remain so. But the Trashmasters format suggests to me that my dictionary is too specific. Perhaps its golfing definition should have stopped short of specifying "as few shots as possible"; perhaps the scoring game should be just one branch of golf, and not the game itself.

Ultimately, though, the Trashmasters – and all the other competitions in this chapter – remind us that competing isn't solely about winning and losing. Add a little spice to the format and you can have a lot of fun simply by taking part, even if that means risking hypothermia or heatstroke. While fair, groomed courses throw the emphasis on scoring and winning, we can easily lose sight of that. Perhaps it takes a few shots in absurd conditions to remind us why we're out there.

The Pillar Mountain Golf Classic especially proves one other thing; that you can set up a golf course in any terrain you choose. And yet, while playing up a mountain is fairly extreme, it is nothing compared with the golfers who have made golf courses out of entire countries.

112 Miles to the Pin

The closing hole at my home club is nicknamed "Cardiac Hill."
It's not original, or even unusual; there are Cardiac Hills at
uphill eighteenths across the globe. Mercifully, only one person
has ever keeled over on the steep slope – and that was because
he caught his foot in a rabbit scrape. Nevertheless, pace of play
dwindles to a virtual standstill as the round reaches its climax.
Apparently a traditional four-and-a-half-mile course is quite
long enough for most of us, thank you very much.

But not for others. Take American Floyd Rood. Rood made
history in 1964 by turning the whole of the United States into a
golf course. His 3,400-mile journey from Pacific to Atlantic
made him the first man to smite a golf ball clean across the US.
A compulsive recorder, Rood noted the trek had taken him a
year and 114 days. He had covered the distance in 114,737
shots, a figure that included penalties for all lost balls – at
3,511, a commendable one a mile.

This odyssey was something of a Rood awakening, for it
helped resuscitate the concept of long-distance cross-country
golf, relatively common a century ago (see Appendix 1) but
long since forgotten. But it did more than that; in no uncertain

terms it reminded an increasingly exclusive sport that you don't need to head to a private country club to hit a golf ball. Golf could be played anywhere you chose, and Californians Bob Aube and Phil Marrone were two of many golfers to answer that call. Their chosen course took them from San Francisco to Los Angeles, one epic 500-mile hole charting the San Joaquin Valley. It took them sixteen days. Bob and Phil lost a thousand balls between them, a figure that again mysteriously equates to one ball per mile lost.

Today, golfers are increasingly ready to turn an entire country into a giant golf course. One of the most remarkable stories concerns a 36-year-old American from New Hampshire, who woke up one morning and decided to hit a golf ball across Mongolia.

Andre Tolme is on the sixth hole. A mere 44 miles long and with a par of 683, it is one of the shorter holes on the course. Andre is preparing to slug a 3-iron to the summit of a hill when a strange noise brushes his consciousness. A low hum is coming from the other side of the peak, not unlike the 30mph wind that is buffeting him, but deeper, more resonant. And getting louder.

Andre forgets the shot and stares up the hill. The noise reaches its peak at the moment around a hundred horses burst into view at the summit. They are racing straight toward him. As the thunderous dust cloud dashes closer, Andre briefly contemplates being trampled before he has even reached the turn. But when the horses get closer he spots people on them – little people. In the next instant a hundred Mongolian children on horseback flash by him, all hooting like crazed owls. Andre is apparently on a racecourse, not a golf course. Thirty seconds later he is alone again, a mote against the monumental Mongolian Steppe, with just a 3-iron for company.

Tolme resolved to play across Mongolia – sandwiched between China and Russia – after visiting the country on a round-the-world trip. It looked, he decided, like the most perfect natural golf course, albeit on a biblical scale. The wide-open savannahs, or steppes, were thinly grassed and made the perfect fairway. A bunker lay in wait down the left of the "fairway" for hundreds of miles, waiting to gobble a hook – although to label the Gobi Desert a bunker is like calling the Pacific a puddle. A powerful river, the Kherlen, would provide a relentless hazard and help map out his route. There were even holes, in the form of marmot burrows. Tolme describes marmots as "like guinea pigs on steroids, quite cuddly looking until someone tells you they spread Bubonic plague."

So Tolme devised a colossal course that would take him from Choybalsan, near the Chinese border, to Khovd in the west. It worked out at 1,234 miles. With the briefest nod at tradition, he divided the country into eighteen holes. The longest was the thirteenth, at 112 miles a fearsome par 845. Tolme would take a week to play it, losing 20 balls on his way to a scrappy 1096 (251 over par). The shortest hole was to be the third, a mere 35-mile jaunt where Tolme would blitz the par of 694 by shooting 344 (350 under par).

Tolme struck his first shot – a soaring 3-iron – in June 2003. Club selection was easy: the 3-iron was his only weapon. With a 55-pound pack on his back, including water and a tent – his home for the next three months – something had to give. The small-faced 3-iron might not sound like the logical choice for this mid-handicapper. "But I wanted to keep the golf as authentic as possible, with penalties for a lost ball," Tolme explains. "So I needed distance and control. The three-iron was the best compromise."

His momentous round soon settled into a regular if uncomfortable pattern. He carried no watch but was woken every morning by the sun blazing down on his tent, turning the interior into a sauna. Breakfast was usually fermented goat's milk. Then would begin a fifteen-mile thrash through dusty valleys, rocky crags and the driving wind – named Salikh by the locals. "I would pass time between shots by counting the number of steps to the ball, chanting the numbers like a mantra and entering a Zenlike state," he recalls. "It helped me deal with the gnats and mosquitoes that never stopped buzzing round my sweaty brow."

Most days Tolme would spend totally alone. In his solitude he was part amused, part worried to realize he had started talking to himself. "I wasn't sure if it was some kind of subconscious psychological defense mechanism to combat the lack of social contact, or whether I was really losing my mind," he recalls. "I don't think it was really happening, but how do you know when you've got no one to ask?" The notion eventually concerned him enough to appoint a caddie who he would see every morning, lunchtime and evening.

The loneliness of the long-distance golfer was also alleviated by the locals. "Mongolians have an amazing culture of hospitality," says Tolme. "Country folk live in remote shacks called yurts. And because the people are so spread out across the country, complete strangers are welcomed into every house. This is how you learn, how knowledge is passed around. You simply knock on the door, say 'How ya doin'?' and start chatting."

Tolme's trip perplexed the locals. For a start, no one walks in Mongolia because of the huge distances from place to place. Anyone who walks is deemed to be very poor because it implies you can't even afford one horse, which costs under $100. But also, despite the recent construction of two golf courses in Mongolia, it was rare for Andre to come across anyone who recognized the game.

"But they all wanted to try. Mongolians make natural golfers. They grow up riding horses and are naturally very co-ordinated and balanced."

Tolme would be offered food and drink, repaying his hosts by helping out with farm work or giving golf lessons. It was in the yurts that Andre learned about Mongolian food and drink. "The summer drink of choice is *airag*, fermented horsemilk. It tastes like sour fizzy milk with a kick.

"Mongolian cuisine is, I guess, simple. In one yurt I yaffled down a hearty meal of sheep's brains, smeared on liver. Another time a family had slaughtered a goat for me. I was tucking into this bit of food that looked like a sausage. A young Mongolian girl who spoke English looked at me with a perfectly straight face and said, 'That's rectum.' It tasted like Italian sausage and calamari. Admittedly, the food gets better with the vodka the locals plied me with."

All the time Tolme was getting further west, hitting the ball off the ground but using preferred lies. Scoring was erratic: he breezed the 44-mile sixth with a convincing 247-under-par total of 436, but gave 255 shots back to the course on the 86-mile eighth. "You couldn't predict anything," he laughs. "Conditions were too chaotic."

The one predictable factor was fatigue. It was hard going. Despite hardy hiking boots, Tolme's feet were blistering; his pack made his back and shoulders ache. But it was even tougher mentally.

"The hardest thing was simply the idea of having to go long distances day after day," he groans. "You can handle a weekend hike, but to plan your route out night after night, to say to yourself, "Right, tomorrow I've got to walk all day long in the flies and the sun and the wind, hitting a golf ball . . ." For the first week all I thought about was quitting, from getting up to going to bed. It probably wasn't until the third week that I went twenty-four hours without wanting to stop."

Nevertheless, Tolme ploughed on stoically until mid-July. He had been hoping to finish before the heavy autumn rains came but they arrived early, turning his clipped fairways into weed beds full of lethal nettles. Progress was impossible and he was forced to put the remaining eight holes and 600 miles on hold until the following spring. He returned to Mongolia in May 2004, completing the course in 44 more windswept and gruelling days. Overall, the 1,234-mile course took him a total of 90 days.

Tolme had set himself a par of 11,880, and in the light of that his final score of 12,170 – 290 over par – might sound a little careless. But criticism would be churlish. That's a tough par. 11,880 works out at 10 shots per mile, or 170 yards per shot – and it's not easy to keep that going over 90 days, especially while being munched by mozzies and attacked by Salikh.

Inevitably, the question Tolme is asked most often is, "Why did you do it?" "I have always loved golf and loved traveling," he muses. "People have climbed mountains, kayaked rivers and cycled the roads of the world, but no one had ever performed a golf expedition before. Golf is an individual test of one man against nature, playing outside in the elements and therefore the perfect sport for a cross-country expedition. I decided I wanted a focused adventure, and what better way than by combining my two passions?

"Plus, Mongolia is an extraordinary place, and this is a wonderful way of learning about another country and another culture. I remember lying in my tent one night and realizing that in one day I had learned how to shear sheep and hobble a horse. I had enjoyed the warm hospitality of two Mongolian families, ate their food, played golf and soccer with them. It was days like this that make the hardships of this long-distance trek worthwhile."

Tolme's arduous quest appears to prove that if there's one thing the long-distance golfer needs, it's fitness. Yet it's now possible to play an 850-mile golf course in South Australia without having to walk any further than you would at your home track.

The course, known as Nullarbor Golf Links, has been set up to follow the Eyre highway, which runs east–west through a treeless, desolate region known as the Nullarbor Plain – a former sea bed. The area is flat enough to allow an arrow-straight 300-mile section of railway – and a 91-mile stretch of road that runs perfectly parallel to it. The Eyre Highway is the main route from Adelaide to Perth, and the car journey is an "I-Spy" fan's worst nightmare – thirty hours with nothing to look at save sky, scrub and, occasionally, sea.

But the new golf course is set to relieve the boredom. By chance there are eighteen towns and roadhouses dotted along this remote stretch of road. Motorists are invited to pull up, play a hole, get back in their car and drive along the highway to the next town and hole – a distance that could be up to sixty miles. A full eighteen-hole round at Nullarbor Golf Links will take you through three time zones.

Each stop on the course promotes a local treasure, which could easily be missed by just bombing ahead. It could be whale-watching just 500 yards from the highway, ancient fossil beds, or even the site where the U.S. Skylab satellite came crashing to Earth in 1979.

"We've even got a hole at Fraser Range, which is a working sheep station," adds Alf Caputo, secretary of the Eyre Highway Operators Association. "So people would be able to have a look at what a sheep station's like." Caputo has also obtained permission from a local Aboriginal community to route a hole through their lands. "The Yalata Aboriginal community is supportive of the concept. This course will showcase the region's history and culture to international tourism, and the Aboriginal community is an important part of our coast."

The idea for the course came from Bob Bongiorno, manager of one of the roadhouses en route. He hopes to combine his love of golf with his hopes of boosting tourism. "I brought my golf clubs when I first came out here seven years ago and tried hitting a few balls in the bush," he says. "But I had to fight the spiders to get them back. I ended up giving the clubs away."

While four of the course's fairways will be grassed, the rest are dirt; the greens will be Astroturf surfaces, and near each one you will find barbecue facilities. It may lack country-club sophistication, but it certainly provides a unique experience for golfers. Says Bongiorno, "Even if people only play a few holes, it will break up their journey. Above all, it will give them the chance to say they've played on the world's biggest golf course."

But of course, you don't have to travel to play long-distance golf; if you so choose, the quest can start right outside your doorstep. A desire to find out more about his homeland was one of the reasons Scotsman David Ewen took up the challenge to play across the country that gave golf to the world. "It dawned on me that I knew more about the life of a lion than a cow or a sheep," he smiles. "I realized I had a lot to learn about Scotland."

Ewen, a reporter for his local Aberdeen newspaper, set off on a bright evening in May 2000. Starting on the east coast, he teed off from the surf of Foveran Beach, water lapping around his feet. His goal was Loch Leven, 160 miles to the west. Like Tolme, he played east–west to avoid hitting into the morning sun, and divided the trip into eighteen "holes" – stretches of countryside ranging from three-and-a-half to twenty miles. If allowed to tee up his ball, Tiger Woods could cover this distance in around 250 blows; Ewen, faced with the dual disadvantage of not being able to use a tee and not being Tiger Woods, awarded himself a par of 10,000, based on an estimate that he would take around sixty shots a mile. It sounds generous until you realize the obstacles and terrain to be conquered – forests and fells, rivers and ravines, Britain's biggest mountain range and fields full of killer cows.

Yes, killer cows. "Scottish cows are quite aggressive," understates Ewen. "They kill four or five farmers a year." His first taste of bovine bother came as early as his sixteenth shot, when a thrilling slice sent his ball into a field full of cattle. He asked the farmer for permission to play through. After bluntly enquiring, "Hiv ye nithin better tae dae wi' ye time?" the farmer set him on his way – but with a chilling augury: "A coo will tak' yer life. I've had my ribs broken afore noo."

Ewen's desire to find out more about his native beasts did not extend to a close-up examination of hoofs and horns. There is a rule in golf allowing a free drop from a dangerous situation, and it was time to take advantage of it. He dropped a second ball, nudging it down a narrow path between two hedges until he could let rip into a field full of comfortingly craven sheep.

As his odyssey progressed Ewen began to lose count of the number of balls claimed by the rough terrain; he would ultimately estimate he lost more than 500. And this despite a carefully worked-out ball strategy: "I interchanged between a golf ball, a tennis ball and a soccer ball. A tennis ball was best on any hard surface, like a road. Even on what appears to be a flat road a golf ball kicks off like a rubber ball, jumping all over the place and ending up in a ditch. I would use the soccer ball on terrain where the tennis ball or golf ball would have disappeared under heather or rocks. The soccer ball's flight was very dependent on wind direction."

Ewen sported a photographer's flak jacket, which he was able to stuff full of as many as a hundred balls every morning. He carried a pencil bag with three clubs – putter, 7-iron and 5-wood. Going light was clearly an advantage but Ewen did wonder if it was going to backfire as he played through the Lairig Ghru, a high and rocky mountain pass in the Cairngorms. "The ground was very stony and compacted and I was worried the heads were going to break. Fortunately they didn't."

Access across Scotland was easier than expected. Ewen, respectful of land ownership but also aware of his right to roam (there is no trespass rule in Scotland), constantly sought permission before playing through. In part, his journey is a reminder of the freedom Scots currently enjoy. With land reform laws in the pipeline and ever-increasing claims on Scottish turf, this might not always be the case.

"As soon as you say you *can* walk here, you instantly designate areas where you *can't* walk," he argues. "The very fact that I was able to cross Scotland virtually unchallenged, swinging a golf club, without upsetting anyone shows that we seem to have got the balance right now. You don't have a God-given right to walk in areas owned by other people, but folks like to roam free and we need to be aware of that, be understanding of that desire, and perhaps relax attitudes a bit."

Ewen even found himself able to golf past the Queen's bedroom after gaining permission to play through the grounds of Balmoral – the Royals' Scottish retreat. "The security guard was fairly relaxed about it," he recalls. "He looked me up and down but let me through. I had the tennis ball out because there was a road up through Balmoral. But beyond the castle I went back to a golf ball. Maybe they hadn't realized I had real golf balls on me."

In fact, throughout his entire journey Ewen only had one problem with access – from golf clubs. While plotting his itinerary he wrote to six courses, asking if he could use their holes as part of his journey. One said yes; the other five did not even reply.

Ewen admits to being a golf fanatic but is no great admirer of golf culture: "I don't belong to a club; I play on public courses. My experience of private clubs has, on the whole, not been great. It's often very cliquey, chauvinistic. The fact that only one in six bothered to reply says it all really, though I guess it's possible that they saw me as an idiot – perhaps not unreasonably – and out to mock or debunk the game of golf. Which, of course, I wasn't."

Despite this Ewen pressed on west, enjoying the spontaneity of following where the ball took him. The golf was different – there was no hole for starters – but perhaps not so far removed from a normal game. "It's like target golf," he declares. "Even though there were open spaces, you still wanted to stick to paths or avoid rocky outcrops and the little lochans. It certainly wasn't mindless slugging."

Ewen made his journey alone. He describes the peace he got from not having to interact with people as "a break from your own voice." He found himself simply responding to what was around him rather than being introspective all the time. "I think being comfortable with your own company is a good thing," he says, "and this journey showed me that I am. I'm quite happy walking on my own. Golf can be a solitary game but when you look at the rules of golf they don't really recognize the lone golfer. Yet for me some of the best moments are when you are on your own, maybe out early, playing the holes you want to play, trying a putt over and over."

Ewen arrived at Loch Leven after eighteen days of hitting golf, tennis and soccer balls toward the setting sun. After having his ball blessed by the local reverend, he belted his final shot gleefully into the Loch. It was his 9,434th blow; he had smashed par by 566 shots.

None of which explains what possesses a sane 36-year-old to suddenly decide to strike out across his homeland, chasing a little white ball. Or sometimes a big red one. Even Ewen doesn't seem entirely sure. But it might have been the spirit of Scotland.

"I no longer think of a field as just a field. I know more about how it supports and affects livelihoods, that sort of thing. I was quite ignorant about history too. I now have a keener understanding of why things are as they are. I have an understanding of what's around me. It's put me in touch with what's under my feet."

It's also put Ewen back in touch with his childhood. "I still remember the thrill of the very first golf shot I hit. I was ten. As a kid I used to jump into a farmer's field and hit balls.

"Maybe I wanted to get back to being a kid. When you're a kid you hit the ball for the love of it. There's a lack of inhibition. When you become an adult you get caught up in rules, in scoring and so on. And you kind of lose the essential thrill, which is swinging the club and getting the ball to launch miles into the sky – if you're lucky. It's getting back to the pleasure of striking the ball; it's being comfortable with your own company; it's not being hung up on what people think; it's about finding pleasure in very simple things.

"Also it took ten shots off my game. When I set off my handicap was 28. When I finished it was 18. I guess it comes from the discipline of hitting 9,000-odd shots. Long-distance golf is great for your game, though I guess this is an extreme way of going about it."

Hitting 9,000 shots is bound to bring your game on a notch, but cross-country golf could be good for your golf in another, more cerebral, way. Ewen and Andre Tolme both faced a lengthy succession of shots to nowhere in particular; a straight shot would very often bring no more reward than a wayward one. There was no out-of-bounds, no awkward bunkers or encroaching lakes . . . they had a whole country to aim at. Relieved of the regular hazards that tie most of us in knots the moment we set foot on the course, they were able to swing with the freedom and confidence of a tour pro.

It's the ideal state of mind for golf, but unfortunately the state is as elusive as it is lucid. A golfer's biggest enemy is himself; we are quite capable of psyching ourselves out of success at any moment. Happily, I was once shown an excellent remedy. Chuntering away to myself after finding yet another way to sabotage my round, I was given some strange advice by a friend, who had watched me implode. "Turn around," he said. "Just hit a ball out there."

Behind the tee was nothing but the North Sea. In a shot reminiscent of Ewen's final blow into Loch Leven, I smote the ball to a watery grave. It was the best swing and strike I'd made all day, aided no doubt by a sudden and profound release from the tension I'd felt. I couldn't miss the sea; and with such a wide target to aim at, I inevitably hit the ball dead straight.

It may have been too late to save that round, but it taught me an important lesson about the state of mind I should be looking to attain on the golf course – you might almost say a cross-country spirit.

Ewen and Andre Tolme are very different people completing very different journeys, but they have much in common. Like Ewen, Tolme quickly grasped the liberating benefits of breaking free from the scorecard. "When you're on your own, hitting a ball across a country, you tend to do a lot of thinking," he says. "You can do that on a normal golf course but your thinking tends to get caught up with your score. Without that to worry about you can appreciate the geology, the wildlife, the people, how it all fits together and how it works. That helped me understand the land."

Also like Ewen, Tolme wanted his magnificent journey to prove to the world that golf should be, and can be, an accessible game. "I hope that I showed that golf can be played anywhere in the world," he adds. "If you love the game then you can play, without belonging to a fancy country club." This genuine quest for the freedom to roam is embedded in each man's psyche, and it is fitting they should choose golf – so often associated with privacy and exclusion – to make their points.

Long-distance golf also flags up another of the game's forgotten assets – the fact that golf is very good for your health. A regular, walking round of golf on a four-mile course burns off about 2,000 calories, so we can only imagine the fitness benefits of cross-country play. Both Ewen and Tolme report having more energy at the end of their exhausting journeys than they did at the start.

Regarded by the uninitiated as a gentle, walking game, golf is in fact a very taxing sport. But that hasn't stopped other maverick players exploring exciting and unorthodox ways to intensify golf's unsung physical side.

Flattening Grooves in Ten Shots

The world will tell you that golf is a game for old people. They will point to the number of American retirement communities set up around golf courses. They will inform you that the average age of the British club member is 57. According to the American wit and *New York Times* columnist Franklin Pierce Adams, "Middle age occurs when you are too young to take up golf and too old to rush up to the net."

Of course, there's something in that. Golf is one of the few outdoor sports that you can play walking, which makes it ideal for older folk. And yet, golf is an intensely physical game. There are 400 muscles and 70 joints in your body, and your swing uses every one – more than once, if you're not careful. A modern golf course is up to five miles long, often scaling rugged terrain. In an average round of golf you will burn off eight calories a minute – that's 2,000 over the course of a four-hour round. That's more than playing two hours of soccer.

Thanks to the physical training regimens of the likes of Tiger Woods and Ernie Els, tour pros are finally and rightly recognized as athletes. But even they are couch potatoes compared to the new breed of golfer bent on taking the physical challenges of the game to the max. So far from being a gentle and slow game, golf for these people is a dynamic, adrenalin-packed sport. As their activities grow in credibility and popularity, the world might just have to revise its opinions of the game and the people who play it.

It's not quite dawn at California's Lomas Santa Fe golf course. Visibility is barely eighty yards, yet on the first tee two furtive figures are gearing up to start a round. Their attire is marathon-runner-meets tour-pro – golf shirts, shorts, running shoes and stopwatches. Each has a pencil bag, holding four clubs only.

The pair strike their opening iron shots simultaneously. In the next heartbeat they are charging down a dusky and dewy fairway, as if trying to catch the balls. In two minutes they are on the green. In nineteen they reach the turn. The round ends within forty minutes of its start. Looking round, they see their vehicles are still the only ones in the car park. The first tee remains empty, so they start again.

By 8.30 a.m. Bob Babbitt, at 54 the publisher of fitness magazine *Competitor*, is at his desk sipping orange juice – and trying to focus on work rather than reflecting on the 36 holes of golf he has just played. He fails. "Let me tell you something," he confides. "If you want to play speed golf, it's a good idea to be first out on the course. When you're running between shots you really don't want to be stuck behind a foursome of old fogeys."

Speed golf, given the patented title of Xtreme Golf, is a simple fusion of running and golf. You jog, you hit, you jog, you hit. Your score is the sum of minutes plus strokes – in this game a score of 120 is very handy. The ideal speed golfer is therefore very good and very fit, although it's better to be an accomplished player than a fast runner. "I'm fitter than a lot of guys I play against," says Babbitt's dawn partner Paul Huddle, a former triathlete but serial 100-shooter in the regular game. "But it doesn't do me much good when I'm zigzagging up the fairway. I'm probably running twice as far as them."

But if the concept of speed golf is easy to digest, it is nevertheless hard for some golfers to stomach. One of the first things you notice about golf is the paint-drying pace of the game; we're supposed to smell the flowers, not hurdle them.

"You don't have to run flat out to enjoy Xtreme golf," Huddle insists. "A fast walk is just as good. The important thing is to keep moving. The principal rule of speed golf is that you cannot delay for anything other than taking a shot. You're either playing or running. It makes you realize how much faffing around is involved in the normal game. Once, we teed off with two fourballs waiting to start behind us. I'm not kidding, when we came up the eighteenth the second group was still on the tee."

Even so, the words "speed" and "golf" go together like "crocodile" and "cuddly." Why make the game faster?

"For one thing, it's very good for you," answers Huddle. "Running a round of golf is a great workout. But there is also a time issue. I was playing regular golf twice a year. I loved it but I never had four or five hours free to play. So this is a great way to get in my jogging fix and my golfing fix."

"People are busy these days," agrees Babbitt. "I think the reason a lot of people don't play golf at all is because it takes too long. Xtreme Golf is perfect for those folks. Plus, even if you play lousy, you're getting in a workout. There's no negative."

Even, it seems, when it comes to the quality of your play. If you thought golfing on the hoof would rip your game to shreds, prepare for a shock. Speed golfers routinely find their golf improves.

Babbitt has a theory: "Xtreme Golf makes your game reactionary. It's a natural thing to react to hitting a ball, but in normal golf you have so much time and you're denied that. You stand there and think through a process. You worry, you fret, you analyze – and usually overthink. There's no time for any of that with speed golf. You're up, you've got to hit. It turns you into an athlete again, gets your instinctive juices flowing."

There is even some evidence to suggest speed golf improves your technique. "Go to see any instructor and one of the first things he'll say is, 'You need loose, relaxed arms,'" adds Babbitt. "That's exactly what you get when you've run a mile. It makes your swing more fluid when you're running. I definitely hit the ball crisper."

Babbitt scoffs at the suggestion that you get tired and lose co-ordination. "Actually I think it's the opposite. A lot of times you try to hit the ball too hard. When you are a little fatigued, you run up and think, oh, I'll just let the club do the work."

Babbitt may have a point here. Casey Sander, who starred in *Grace Under Fire*, played in one of Babbitt's celebrity events and reported he had never driven so well because he was so worn out. "I could do no more than swing the club back and through," he gasped afterwards. "I couldn't overswing."

The rules of Xtreme Golf are exactly the same as for the traditional game – with the exception that you can leave the flag in to putt. It's the etiquette that sees the diversion. The usual do-you-minds and after-yous are forgotten. You tee off when you're ready, even if that means at the same time as your playing partner. You don't wait to hit in the fairway either, even when someone is weaving across your path ahead. "You just shout, 'Incoming!'" laughs Babbitt.

It sounds dangerous but Huddle denies it. "OK, I have been hit once," he admits. "In the back of the leg. But that was simply because I was playing with someone who wasn't very good. I was five feet in front and thirty feet to the right and he caught one out of the toe. "But if there's someone in your line, you can just take a split second and wait. It may be called speed golf, but it's not so very frantic."

Babbitt and Huddle are by no means the first speed golfers. Dick Kimbrough famously set a world record in 1972 by playing North Plate, Nebraska in 30 minutes and 10 seconds. But it took the intervention of the great American miler Steve Scott to add luster to running golf. In 1979 Scott broke Kimbrough's record, playing round in 29 minutes and 30 seconds. At this breakneck speed Scott still managed to break 100, shooting a 95.

Scott helped shape the modern era of running golf by competing in a made-for-TV event in 1994, staged by Bob Babbitt and screened by ESPN. Babbitt's masterstroke was to bring back the ability element into playing fast by introducing the minutes-plus-shots scoring system. The event was a success. It led to the Powerbar Xtreme Golf Open and put speed golf on the map.

By 1998 a group called Speedgolf International had taken over the mantle of promoting running golf. Headed by former pro Tim Scott, it holds twice-yearly events in Oregon and Illinois. But despite the ease with which it can be played, and the undoubted universal appeal of both running and golf, Xtreme Golf remains very much a niche activity.

"Golf is a traditional game and there is a lot of traditional thinking," reckons Huddle. "This is not what you think of when you imagine a game of golf. I'd equate it to snowboarding. Initially there was a lot of resistance from traditional skiers, but before you knew it full mountains were doing it. I reckon the same thing will happen with Xtreme Golf. But it needs to reach a level of popularity first, and at the moment there's too much traditional thinking out there."

"It hasn't really caught on yet – though I think it will," says Babbitt. "People see it as paying a hundred-buck green fee for an hour, but you can do it at an executive course like we do and pay ten dollars.

"Also, the more conservative clubs think we are going to tear up the course, which of course we don't. We replace divots, rake bunkers, repair ball marks. We don't run on the greens. Believe me, we do less damage than a 250-pound giant dragging his cleats along the grass.

"I think there are a lot of purists in golf who look at us and think it's a freak show or it's weird. True, speed golf doesn't immediately make a lot of sense. But for me that's part of the attraction. You can bring in DJs, get music going, put your opponent off . . . it's kind of the anti-golf, with the emphasis on fun and fitness, not score.

"Look at it this way. This morning I got to play thirty-six holes before work and I hit twenty good shots in an hour. I can't remember ever doing that during a regular game."

While we may not all wish to hurtle around the golf course in forty minutes, speed golf can teach us a thing or two about slow play – a disease that has infected the regular game in recent years. Like many golfers, I have come to expect five-hour rounds in local club competitions. This is virtually twice as long as the average round of golf took fifty years ago.

Perhaps we can blame TV. We have all watched our hero tour pros painstakingly plot their way around the golf course, taking umpteen yardages and reading putts from seventeen angles – and inevitably, we have copied them. But while they are playing to put food on the table for their families, we are playing for fun and recreation.

The irony is that all our extra care and attention makes us play worse. Slow play doesn't just stop us getting into a rhythm; as Bob Babbitt points out, too much thinking time counts against the amateur, haunted as he is by the inadequacies of his game. We would do better to make our playing of the game more instinctive, to make better use of our natural ball-striking skills. Faster play would deny us the opportunity to psyche ourselves out of the shot. All we have to do is accept that we are not Tiger Woods.

Speed golf also flags up the importance of warming up before the round. Nobody would envision sprinting off from cold, but in a golfing sense that is exactly what most players do. The rules don't help us here; in strokeplay events we are not allowed on to the course before the round starts. For traditional golfers a pre-round warm-up might consist of a few putts, some chip shots, maybe even some full-out swings if there's a range handy.

But if you're preparing for a round of mountain golf, you might want to try a different approach.

"I'd start with aspirin," nods Californian Ric Moore, a PGA pro and a former champion of the UX Open – the world's foremost mountain golf event. "I will try to knock back 800mg before a round. At altitude your blood tends to coagulate, but I've found aspirin helps keep my blood thin enough for me to think and function properly. I also drink loads more than usual because the thin air dehydrates you."

Mountain golf is the game that can have you literally swinging on cloud nine. Events are held on summer ski slopes across the USA, typically at heights of more than 10,000 feet above sea level. At Snowmass, Aspen they play at 12,000 feet, while in Mammoth, California, it's 11,000. The courses may be only ten holes long but the average length of each hole is 538 yards – and that's not always downhill. The longest hole in UX Open history weighed in at 1,220 yards.

And although a pretty swing won't exactly harm your chances of success, your physical resilience is what makes or breaks you. Moore quickly learned the importance of coping with altitude during his first UX Open in 2002, when he finished third.

"I was unable to find the strength to finish the tournament off," he recalls. "I had shortness of breath and a horrible feeling of laziness and lethargy. Every step was a major labor. The last thing you want to do is swing a golf club.

"So I spoke to doctors in the mountains about the effects of altitude and how to combat them. They told me the body has a 24-hour period where you can play in altitude unaffected. But after those 24 hours it takes two weeks for your body to become acclimated. So I needed short-term fixes to keep my energy levels up, and I think they've worked; in 2003 I finished second, and in 2004 I won."

It's not just the thin air that makes winning at mountain golf as much a feat of endurance as skill. Terrain varies from mountain to mountain – at Snowmass you need to cope with thick, lush grass; at Mammoth it's slippery and unstable pumice. But wherever you are, you must deal with rocks, forests, canyons and waist-high grass – and that's before you start to figure out the abrupt contours on which you must somehow manage to perch.

And it's here that Moore reveals a second secret strategy for slope success – a cunning training program based on, of all things, motocross.

"Imagine trying to keep a motorcycle upright around jumps

and obstacles and corners, on dirt," he says. "You are working every balance muscle in your body. Balance is a key skill of mountain golf. And it is great stamina training; if you can go for twenty minutes as fast as you can, you feel like you've just run a marathon. Trust me, I do it twice a month."

There are two friendly rules to mountain golf. First, you always get to drop your ball within a club-length of its lie without penalty, and second, there is no putting – you've finished the hole when your ball ends up in a 25-foot circle. Apart from that, it's all hard. And the challenge is pumped up by a four-club limit.

"You've got to pick the right clubs and use them to the max," reckons Moore. "Most people think you should choose driver because of the huge distances and open spaces. But I take a three-wood for maximum carry. When the ground is rough, you want the ball in the air. Plus it is versatile – I could use it on the fairway. For the irons I choose four-iron, six-iron, nine-iron and manipulate them by opening or hooding the face, choking down, altering the swing, adjustments an advanced player would make."

Even this doesn't always help. At one stage in 2002 Moore's ball was lying in a deep depression and the only decent lie he could give himself within one club-length was on top of a rock. Clenching anything that would clench, he picked a 9-iron, shut his eyes and swung. The ball found the circle, but the 9-iron ended up in two pieces. "If you have nice golf equipment this is the last place you want to bring it," he says.

A mountain golfer wears hiking boots for ankle support on the treacherous terra-not-so-firma, and sports several layers of clothing to adapt to the mountain-weather mood swings. A round in this exacting environment can take up to six hours, but 46-year-old Moore never has a problem trading the groomed fairways of California's Bakersfield Country Club, where he is director of golf, for the wilds.

"The normal game is great but it doesn't always give you that adrenalin rush," he says. "I like things that challenge me. That's why I still do motocross and snowboarding. I play mountain golf for the challenge of maintaining good balance, surviving the elements and tackling tough situations."

Mountain golf also has a freedom that keeps Moore radiant on the gradient. "Traditional golf would call it a lack of reverence," he says, "but when you're out in the mountains you can whoop and holler and feel alive and vibrant. If you hit a well-struck golf shot you can let out a big yell and hear your voice echoing in the hills. It would be poor etiquette on a regular golf course, but we feed off that energy. If you feel your golf – or your life – is bound by rules and structure, then this is a great outlet. It allows you the chance to release yourself for a short time."

One way all golfers gain a feeling of release – as well as an adrenalin surge – is by setting out to hit the ball as hard as possible.

Unfortunately, our concept of the scoring game denies us the opportunity to experience this too often. We all grudgingly accept that, when it comes to a golf score, accuracy is going to help us more than distance – a 300-yard drive is no good to you if it sends the ball out-of-bounds. Nudging the ball into position may be the smart play, but it doesn't half make for a tedious round of golf.

This leaves the power-hungry golfer with two options; either get the driver out, give it a ride and to hell with the score, or enter the arena of professional long driving. Long-drive contests are springing up all over the world, with twenty every year in the States alone. The rise of power golf as an independent sport owes a lot to Arkansas-born Sean Fister.

Born in 1962, Fister has been at the forefront of the movement that has seen long driving develop from a talking point to a sport in its own right. A three-time winner of the ReMax World Long Driving Championship, he has been competing for nineteen years and has been a professional, full-time hitter for ten.

"My clubhead speed at impact was once measured at 171.2 miles per hour," Fister drawls, somehow managing to sound bored and impressed at the same time. Tiger Woods' clubhead speed with the driver averages out at 122mph. "It takes me about ten shots for the grooves in the face of my driver to disappear."

Normal golfers, who drive the ball perhaps 260 to 270 yards and have a clubhead speed of around 100mph, will find Fister's formidable feats of force hard to fathom. He is what you might call a natural; he didn't touch a club until he was 25. Then, in his first ever round, he drove the green on a 342-yard par-four. Since then he has just got longer. Fister has found himself putting for albatross (double eagle) five times. "I only converted two of them," he rues. On one of those occasions the putt was one foot long; Fister was twelve inches away from a hole-in-one on a par-five, a feat so improbable it doesn't even have a name. His average drive is 350 yards, but when he wants to, and he is swinging well, he can put another hundred on top of that.

He also has the unfortunate habit of destroying the face of his titanium driver.

"At the 2005 World Championships I took twenty-eight heads with me. After two days of practice I had caved them all in. I had to call my wife to send me another twenty-five. All in all I went through forty driver heads. It'd be getting expensive if they weren't sponsored."

Mind you, a day of practice is different in FisterWorld. "I'm a marathon hitter. I'll hit a thousand balls with driver alone. It takes about seven hours, with a break for lunch. And I will usually do that every day for three months before a championship." His target is to make his last ball his longest hit of the day.

There are two questions everyone asks Sean Fister: "How do you do it?" and "Why aren't you on tour?" He is more forthcoming on the latter. "You know, I used to train for decathlon, but I was only really any good at pole vault. Tour pros are like decathletes; they can do everything well. They have the sand game, the knockdown shot off a tight lie . . . there's so much more to golf. The longest hitters out there, John Daly and Tiger Woods, have awesome short games, that never get talked about. I guess I am a specialist, not a decathlete."

As regards the secret of power – golf's holy grail – Fister is guarding his secrets, though being six-foot-five and 235 pounds clearly doesn't hurt. "I have some things I do that train my muscles for explosiveness," he admits finally. "I'll tell you about one, simply hitting a heavy bag with a softball bat. I beat the hell out of it. I work on staying behind it and snapping through it. I listen out for the loudest pop. If your hands are early or late, you won't get it; time it just right and you'll hear it."

Despite a muscular frame, Fister doesn't work out, apart from some general conditioning work. He describes the key muscle areas as the shoulder girdle, the arms and the big back muscles. "It's basically the same stuff you'd use to pull a boat up on shore with a rope. It's kind of the same motion, except you're also trying to sling that boat eighty yards out of the water."

Despite his ability to create raw power, Fister relegates it behind technique in long-hitting importance. "Long drives are forty-five percent power, fifty-five percent technique," he reckons. "You can have all the power in the world and not hit it out of your own shadow."

While Fister is very much the present of power hitting, its godfather is Englishman Mike Austin. Austin struck the longest golf shot ever hit in competition as a 64-year-old – and with a wooden-headed driver. At the 1974 National Seniors Open he smote a phenomenal blow of 515 yards. The ball finished 65 yards past the green on a long par-four. It remains the longest drive ever recorded in competition. Eyewitnesses describe the shot as "like God was holding the ball in the air."

Austin's action – a vigorous leg drive coupled with a strange casting of the clubhead – was considered ahead of its time by experts. He broke the 400-yard barrier at 27 and took great joy in organizing power stunts. Once he drove a ball through the Los Angeles phone book; another time he hit a ball more than 200 yards with a taped-up cola bottle. His clubhead speed at impact was once measured at 155mph – 33 faster than Tiger's average.

Technique is also vital to professional long hitters in that there is an accuracy element to the competition – you can't just crunch it. In the ReMax World Championship, the winner must get through seven rounds. In each round he lets rip at six balls, which must finish within a fifty-yard wide zone to count. "You win those things by having the mechanics to hit the ball accurately time after time after time," says Fister. "That's why my own technique has evolved from a hitter to a swinger. I started out with an extremely violent golf swing but I have learned to swing faster and not harder, making good contact. I can make a louder pop on my heavy bag if I relax and just sort of sling the bat into it. It works with golf too. That's how I carried it 393 yards through the air in the 2005 ReMax semis.

It's about speed, not effort."

In winning the 2005 ReMax, Fister pocketed $100,000. He also makes $10–15,000 by playing in exhibitions and pro-ams. But the cash is not the main attraction. "Why do I do it? I guess it's the shock, the looks on people's faces when I hit it. I once hit in front of President Clinton, and he couldn't say anything. He just laughed, a real belly laugh.

"I hit in front of Tiger once, too. The ball flew off and smacked a tree. It brought down a branch that was about four inches across. He just grinned at me. I've had some great comments too. Tommy Bolt, the 1958 U.S. Open winner, once said that if he had hit it that far, no one would have heard of Arnold Palmer. More normally folk say things like, 'I had no idea a golf ball could be hit that far'. Or they say they've never heard the sound that the ball makes with a golf club. It reminds me of the fact that I am able to do something that people very rarely get to see. That's the kind of stuff that I feed off."

Everyone who has ever played golf knows the childlike pleasure of hitting the ball as hard as possible – but there may well be some more grown-up psychology wrapped up in that great feeling a power drive gives us. "Culturally there is a bias toward the big hitter," says sports psychologist Dr Karl Morris, who works with tour pro Darren Clarke and co-authored the bestselling book *The Mind Factor* with the Ulsterman. "It's almost a sin to be a good putter; hole a few putts and you're seen as lucky, streaky. But knock the dimples off the ball and you're a hero. You are a leader, a gladiatorial type. It's the same in other sports. You could probably name half a dozen great heavyweight boxers, but no one remembers the bantamweights."

Morris believes we are like this because our brains are still wired into ancestral thought patterns, developed over thousands of years of hunter-gathering. "The guy who smashes it miles is the one who would have reeled in the wildebeest or the sabre-toothed tiger. The "feel" you need to slide in a downhill left-to-right putt is not going to feed, clothe and protect your family."

Yet it's into the testosterone-charged, ego-fueled world of slugging a golf ball that a tall, slim, blonde woman has arrived. Californian Stacey Shinnick has won the Remax Women's Long Drive World Championship three times since its inception in 2000. Stacey averages a little over 300 yards off the tee, regularly nudging the 350-yard barrier in general play. Her winning blow in the 2005 ReMax Long Drive measured in at 311 yards.

Stacey outdrives the men on a regular basis – and some of them don't like it. "On a few occasions I've had guys walk off after the first couple of holes," Stacey smiles. "They say they're not feeling well. And maybe they're not – I can't read minds – but it does seem to happen quite often!"

According to Stacey, if you want some extra firepower off the tee, get into yoga. "I started doing yoga two years ago," she says. "My boyfriend brought me a tape called "Yoga for Golfers." At first I thought it was a bit of a gimmick; but as soon as I tried it, I knew I had really found something. Ever since, I've hit the ball so much better. I would say it has added maybe twenty yards to my tee shots. I feel such a difference in terms of relaxation and flexibility. It sounds a bit New Age and mystical but if you think of it as golf-specific stretching, it doesn't seem so bad. It helps me make a full shoulder turn. And in normal golf I don't feel tight on the last few holes."

More Barbie than Barbarian, Stacey is not your archetypal power hitter. "I wouldn't say I was a girly girl," she says, "but

I'm still very feminine. I don't see that you have to sacrifice that to be a powerful hitter. Long-drive events may not seem the thing for a woman to do, but I do it because I love the competition – and because I'm pretty good at it."

But despite Shinnick's achievements, women's power golf languishes some way behind men's. While there have been male world long-drive championships since 1975, the first ladies" event did not appear for a further 25 years. And although gear company Pinnacle sponsored a tour of eight televised events for women in 2004, they pulled out in 2005 – leaving competitions few and far between. The gulf is reflected in the prize money; in 2005 Sean Fister won $100,000 for scooping the top prize at the ReMax. Stacey's winning blow netted her a tenth of the amount. "I'm a professional long driver," she says, "but it's very hard to earn a living this way. There isn't really a reward for second or third. You have to win."

Our perception is that power golf does not mix with scoring golf, but perhaps it is false. Fister and Shinnick are accurate drivers while golf legend Arnold Palmer is all the evidence we need that smacking the ball hard doesn't have to come at the expense of control. When Arnie was learning the game as a child, his father told him, "Hit it hard, boy. Go find the ball and hit it hard again." It was a lesson Arnold learned well; he even called his first book, released in 1961, *Hit It Hard*.

Inspired by Shinnick and Fister, I set out to play a round of golf in which I let fly at every full shot. My shots were no less and no more accurate, but they were, when I got the timing right, a lot longer. What did improve was my enjoyment. My desire to do things "correctly" evaporated; mentally, I was freed up to play golf. The experience reminded me of the simplest and best piece of golf instruction I have ever heard. "After taking the stance it is too late to worry," said Bobby Jones in 1929. "The only thing to do then is to hit the ball."

Playing a spot of power golf is easy; all it takes is a bit of extra loosening up, while entering into a contract pledging to judge the shot not on where the ball ends up but on the arc the ball makes as it sears the sky. It's a much more disinterested criterion, and all the more powerful because of it. This is a form we should be willing to sign more often.

Power hitting may warrant physical strength, but golf is a game that can bring out mental fortitude too. The golfers in the next chapter take golfing courage beyond holing a putt when the match is at stake or coming back from five-down; these are people who owe their very survival to the game of golf.

6

Golf in a Prison Cell

On 2 April 1972 Colonel Iceal "Gene" Hambleton was shot down while flying his 63rd combat mission of the Vietnam War. Ejecting at 31,000 feet, he was the only crew member to make it out alive.

Hambleton was now stuck in the jungle, surrounded by 30,000 enemies and with only a URC-64 survival radio for company. The closest the special operations team could get to pick him up was about four miles away, near the Cam Lo River. They needed a code to navigate Hambleton through hostile territory to the pick-up point, something that could not be understood by the Vietnamese radio monitors. Hambleton lay low for six days, eating whatever he could safely scavenge, until special operations came up with an amazing solution.

Air Force Reserve Colonel Darrel D Whitcomb, who wrote a history of this rescue, recalled: "Members of his squadron told us that he loved golf and had a photo-like memory of holes he'd played. So the team set about organizing an eighteen-hole course that would guide Hambleton around villages and emplacements, safely to the pick-up point."

The first Hambleton knew of it was when his radio picked up instructions to play the first hole at Tucson National, a par four that ran 408 yards southeast. Grasping the meaning, he waited until nightfall before pacing out 400 yards southeast. In this way, and by using holes from several Air Force Base courses and one from Augusta National, the special ops team led Hambleton to the river and safety.

Hambleton had been behind enemy lines for eleven and a half days. During that time he radioed USAF planes to guide them to targets he could see. He earned a Silver Star, Distinguished Flying Cross and a Purple Heart. A 3-handicapper when captured, he golfed into his 86th year, playing every Wednesday up until his death in 2004. His amazing rescue was made into a 1988 film called *Bat-21*, starring Gene Hackman.

For most of us, courage in a golfing context means holing a five-footer for the match on the last – or perhaps landing a delicate pitch within a foot or two of the far side of an abyssal bunker. But Hambleton's experience reveals how golf and courage can fuse in rather more meaningful ways. And as epic as his rescue was, it was not the only time during the Vietnam conflict that golf came to an American's rescue.

As 5-irons go, it's not bad, not good – a slightly heavy contact and a bit of a pull that leaves the ball some thirty yards short of the hole in the semi-rough. It would have been better but for an unlucky kick off a small mound. "Still, the chip doesn't look so tough," thinks George Hall, the player of that apparently ordinary shot.

In fact there is nothing ordinary about it at all. That 5-iron was struck from a dark, tiny cell in a Vietnamese prisoner-of-war camp nicknamed Briar Patch by the American POWs. Hall – or Air Force Captain Hall to give him his full title – is in solitary confinement. He has not seen another prisoner for eight months and is surviving on grey water, a crust of bread and, if he is lucky, watery pumpkin soup. In playing a round a day – always nine in the morning, nine in the afternoon – he is using a game that is supposed to drive people nuts to keep himself sane.

Hall, a USAF reconnaissance photographer, was shot down in September 1965 while taking damage-assessment photos of two bridges near Hanoi. It was his 191st combat mission. Somehow he managed to eject, but no one saw the parachute and his family did not know if he was alive or dead for sixteen months.

Hall was picked up by the Vietnamese and treated by a doctor, who sewed his bitten tongue together and bandaged his right arm. The hospitality ended there; he promptly had a rope thrown around his neck and was dragged through villages, where the locals were encouraged to throw things at him.

After interrogation and beatings Hall, 35 at the time, was forced into the solitary-confinement hell that would be his world for the next eighteen months. He was in a seven-foot-square cell in the "Poolhouse" area of a main prison known as the Zoo. He had no communication with fellow prisoners bar a tapping code, and when he tried it and got caught he was tortured and half-starved. Often he was forced to squat with his hands above his head for hours on end. He was utterly on his own and in danger of losing his mind.

"I was alone and needed some way to mentally get out of there each day," remembers Hall. "My solution was to play dream rounds of golf. I chose golf as a means of escaping the cells because it was my only hobby besides my love of flying. I was a two-handicap when I got captured. Golf also allowed me to remember old friends and the joy of playing with them – and thinking of the many beautiful courses I had played."

So each day Hall would conjure up, in his mind, a course that he had played during a 25-year golfing life that included being captain of the Navy's 1953 golf team. Often this would be his home course at the Hattiesburg Country Club.

"I would act out arriving at the clubhouse, speaking to the pro, even getting a caddie. And then I would be off to the first tee. I would visualize the hole and then hit my drive. Depending on how I hit it, I would take the appropriate number of steps around my cell. Two hundred and forty steps would be the usual drive; it worked out at two-thirty for a three-wood, two-twenty for a two-iron and so on.

"I always made par on each hole. No bogeys or birdies, just pars. For some reason it never occurred to me to shoot under par. That's not to say I hit all perfect shots. I hit a lot of greens in regulation but also made a lot of adventurous pars. I played sand shots and made some long putts. But I always ended up with a par."

Hall would even speak to the people he met on the course. Guards outside his door would hear "Good morning Mr Bethea," and "Nice day, Mrs Foote." "They would open the peephole sometimes to see what was going on," Hall recalls. "They would just shake their heads at my behavior. They didn't understand."

In April 1966 Hall's captors moved him to Briar Patch but kept him in solitary confinement. So Hall kept to his golfing routine. One day, and out of the blue, the guards let him outside briefly. He immediately sought out a four-foot-long stick and smuggled it back into his cell. "I would swing it like a club during my rounds. But one day during a cell shakedown they took it away from me. I felt like I lost my best friend."

Then finally, in September 1966, Hall got a room-mate. "I continued playing golf for a few months after that," he recalls. "But I certainly didn't play as much. I still praticed my swing each day along with some mild exercise, but life was very different with someone to talk to directly."

Hall remembers his first four years in prison as "pure hell – bad food, too little food, no outside exercise, torture, being forced to apologize to the Vietnamese people for flying over their airspace, no letters from home and spending the entire first year in solitary confinement." But in 1970 food and treatment suddenly improved, as rumors of release intensified.

Hall was one of the first American prisoners to be let out, in February 1973 – 7 years and 148 days after his capture. Shortly after his release he played in a pro-am in New Orleans. No doubt inspired by his vivid par-golf visualizing, he shot an impressive 81.

Hall is now a retired Air Force Colonel, and free to visit all those courses he played in his head during that year of hell. He remains a passionate player – even if his current 17-handicap means he cannot quite match that incredible run of par golf.

American entertainer Will Rogers once said, "Golf is great for the soul; you get so mad at yourself, you forget to hate your enemies." But it's unlikely that Colonel George Hall selected golf as his sanity-preserver for this reason. More likely it is the fact that golf, like no other sport, speaks directly to the human spirit. John Updike alluded to this in his book *Updike's Adventures in Golf's Wonderland* when he wrote: "To see one's ball gallop 200 and more yards down the fairway, or to see it fly from the face of an 8-iron clear across an entire copse of maples in full autumnal flare, is to join one's soul with the vastness that, contemplated from another angle, intimidates the spirit and makes one feel small."

Why the game should have this profound effect on us is open to conjecture – and maybe it is best left that way. But certainly golf, a mental and individual game, has always afforded its participants the chance to find out about themselves. The challenges of the game are the challenges of our daily lives – perseverance, courage, honesty, self-control, coping with success and failure. It is not hard to see why a good game of golf, in which all those challenges are met, would give our spirits a tremendous lift. Perhaps this is why our golf game is so tightly knit to our psyches, why a good shot sends us into orbit while bad play eats into our stomachs.

Golf's link with the spirit is surely why people appear to feel a desire to turn to the sport in times of need. For, as golf helped provide the inspiration for Hall's mental survival, so it assisted a Canadian in his quest for physical recovery.

In 1987 Bob MacDermott was in his dad's tractor, cultivating round some wooden poles at the far end of the farm. The poles were supporting cables. Unused to the machinery, MacDermott strayed too close to one and knocked it down. Cross with himself, he got down to pull it out of the way. For some reason, he had it in his head that the cables were phone lines; but they were power lines. The last thing he remembered was approaching them, strewn across the stubbly field.

In the next few seconds MacDermott was hit with 14,500 volts and thrown across the field, landing on his back.

Then MacDermott had his only good luck of the day. Two farmers saw the felled power pole from the road and came over to investigate and found MacDermott lying on the ground. One of them, Jeff Graham, recalls MacDermott was so hot that he was actually sizzling.

They loaded him into a truck and sped to nearby Kindersley Hospital. At the under-equipped Kindersley they prepped MacDermott for the two-hour ambulance drive to Saskatoon. But along the highway the ambulance, doing 80mph, blew a tire. It swerved, causing it to blow a second tire, then rolled and threw MacDermott – who was not strapped in because of his severe skin burns – out the back and into a wheat field.

His brother Rick, following behind, raced across the field, terrified of what he would find. He thought Bob was dead, until his eyes flickered open and he muttered, "Rick, will you get the stubble out of the crack of my butt?"

Bob MacDermott heard sirens and, in a sudden moment of clarity, wondered if he was alive or dead. On the edge of consciousness, he was unaware of the second ambulance that eventually pulled up by the roadside.

"I never actually lost consciousness," says Bob MacDermott today. "Although I did hallucinate. I thought I was still driving the tractor. After the electricity hit me I felt so hot, really sick, kind of like a really bad hangover. I had no idea what had happened till days later."

MacDermott was in hospital for seven weeks – four in the burns unit, three in plastic surgery while they put him back together. In all, 40 percent of his skin was covered in third- and fourth-degree burns. Within four days gangrene was setting in to his left arm and leg. The doctors offered him a choice: limbs or life.

MacDermott lost his left leg below the knee and his left arm below the elbow, as well as his right thumb. It would take nine skin-graft operations to replace the skin he lost. The next weeks were mental and physical hell.

"In hospital my thoughts were consumed by what I was going to be able to do," he says. "The three things that concerned me was whether I could play with my kids again, whether I could work and if I could ever play golf."

Golf was just becoming a major part of MacDermott's life. He is a self-confessed sports nut but barely touched a club until he was thirty. Entranced by the personal challenge of the game, MacDermott got down to a 7-handicap in just two years. By 1987, he felt he could mount a serious challenge for his local club championship. Unfortunately, the event clashed with the day his dad needed help harvesting on his farm.

After the operations MacDermott spent four months in rehab, sitting at home and waiting for the skin to heal. It gave him a chance to think about resurrecting his golf career. His hopes were buoyed by the doctors' assurance that there were prosthetics out there that could help him.

Then he read up about terminal devices, attachments that fit in the end of prosthetic limbs. He saw one in a catalogue that he was sure would allow him to grip a golf club. Developed by prosthetics company Troppman, it consisted of a tubular element that could flex like a wrist and a spoon-like end that fitted over the club's grip, retaining a firm hold.

While the discovery of this terminal device gave him a huge boost, Bob still had to come to terms with his new body and his new life. "I realized I had to start over. I had to learn everything again. How do I pull my pants up? How do I tie my shoes? I had to adapt. Everything was fine in my life with no real issues. It takes something like this to make you realize there's a process to learning to do something – anything. And to do it well you have to set goals."

Bob applied this goal-setting mentality to his golf. His first goal was simply to play. He sought the advice of his club pro at Lloydminster GC, Peter Cushner. "Bob was determined to play again but needed encouragement," recalls Cushner. "I looked at what he had and realized we could create a swing. I was never in doubt that it would work – the harder part was getting him to believe that."

But first there were a few things that needed changing.

"First thing was the artificial left hand and wrist. He had a kind of rigid clamp on the end of his prosthesis. We needed to create a means of letting that artificial wrist hinge so that he could cock the club back as he swung. So we ended up pushing a piece of hose in there between the clamp and the prosthesis. I told Bob simply to use his right arm to cock that left wrist."

After this, Cushner's next step was to change Bob's approach to hitting the ball. "Bob was a powerful man who hit the ball hard with his hands and arms. I told him he could hit the ball just as well through technique, with the body turn producing the centrifugal force. When the body turns well, the club just moves around it; the hands and arms can be pretty passive. In this respect it was the same lesson I'd give to anyone.

"So it became a question of creating a swing driven by body rotation rather than an aggressive hands-and-arms hit."

Bob achieved his first goal of simply playing in April 1988, just eight months after the accident. He shot 89 for nine holes. "My swing was unorthodox and painful," he reflects. "I hit the ball but that was about all you could say about it. That was hard when I had been down to a seven-handicap, to suddenly play to plus forty. Yet I achieved the first goal."

The final step was building a weight transfer back into his swing. For this Bob had to get over the pain and fear of putting weight on his left lower prosthesis. It would take him a further four months of practice and intense pain.

"I would hit three or four bucketloads a day, maybe a hundred and fifty balls. It caused a lot of pain, especially with the follow-through and weight shift," he winces. "Learning to balance was hard. I was getting skin breakdown from overdoing it. There was blood in my sockets. But the desire to go out and play was greater then the pain saying 'Stop'."

MacDermott played on through the pain barrier. The medics knew there was not much stopping him so settled for trying to slow him down. They failed there too. The only thing that would have stopped Bob was an infection, but he took care of himself to make sure that didn't happen, despite the constant skin breakdown that threatened his chances of hanging on to the progress he had made.

Through sheer persistence he started to improve. And once he started, he did not stop. "When I started to see results from the practice I was putting in, it just added fuel to the drive of wanting to get better, to get better than I was before."

MacDermott achieved that goal as well. Amazingly, in two years he was down to a 5-handicap.

"I think the belief that I could do this came initially through my passion for the game," he says. "I always had the drive, but I was just so glad to be playing – I was so glad to be breathing."

The next few years saw MacDermott become the foremost amputee golfer in Canada and America. He won two Canadian National Amputees Championships and five U.S. Amputee Championships. He became a multiple winner of the Alberta Provincial tournament and won the British Amputee Championships in Ireland in 2005. Maybe sweetest of all, he has won three club championships, competing against able-bodied golfers – some revenge for missing out on the event back on that fateful day in 1987.

Today MacDermott manages eleven community homes for people with developmental difficulties in Edmonton. He is also a motivational speaker and the director of the Canadian Amputee Golf Association. He doesn't play as much golf as he would like, but when he does play he walks the eighteen holes, carrying his clubs. He drives the ball an average 280 yards but believes he has to pratice his short game harder to make up for the loss of feel through not having a left hand.

"I still have golfing goals, though," he says. " I want to play more able-bodied tournaments. They build awareness of amputee golf, especially if I do well.

"Plus it helps people realize that when something happens, it's not the end of the world. You can still do a lot of things you were doing before. And sometimes you can do them even better."

Such is the allure of golf that we have all taken to the course when we perhaps shouldn't have done. Australian star Karrie Webb risked being expelled when, as a youngster, she bunked off school to play the neighboring course. German goalkeeper Oliver Kahn risked losing his place in Bayern Munich's team by spending all day playing golf when he was supposed to be resting an injury. In South Korea, Prime Minister Lee Hae-chan risked his job in March 2006 by golfing when he should have been resolving a national railway strike. My own escapades have tended to involve themes of substantial workloads, sudden illnesses and sunny Monday mornings.

Of this disparate foursome only Webb and I got away with it; Kahn and Lee were discovered. In Lee's case, he was already in the dock after an April 2005 incident in which he had golfed as a wildfire destroyed a 1,300-year-old Buddhist temple. He was forced to resign. But what if discovery didn't just cost you your job, but also your life?

If you were to pitch up for a game at Kabul Golf Club, Afghanistan, you would be greeted by a thin, moustached man named Mohammed Abdul Afzal. Afzal, now in his fifties, is the club pro. His shop is a mud hut; the clubhouse, bombed out long ago, houses only goats. But Afzal doesn't care about shops or goats. When you have been tortured and imprisoned for your love of golf, that sort of thing stops bothering you.

Afzal became a pro here in 1971, when the course was built and Afghanistan still had a constitutional monarchy. At the time the place also hosted a yachting marina and was bustling with Kabul's upper classes – Afzal would spend his days giving lessons to ambassadors, dignitaries and diplomats. The course was irrigated, lush and green.

But Afzal's problems started with the Soviet invasion of 1979. The Communists immediately declared golf a Western, capitalist pastime and accused Afzal of liaising with American secret agents. He was beaten and imprisoned for six months. By the time he came out, the golf course wasn't just closed; it was an integral part of a strategic line of defense as the Russians dug in against the freedom-fighting Mujaheddin. There were tanks and howitzers on the fairways, and trenches cut through old green sites.

The battle raged for ten years. During this time Afzal earned a living driving a taxi, but could not forget about playing golf. Every Friday he would collect his secret stash of clubs and drive off in his taxi to a hidden valley and hit balls. If he had been caught, he would almost certainly have been killed.

After the Russians withdrew in 1989, a multi-faction Mujaheddin government took control. In a period of uneasy truces and civil disturbances Afzal was able to take steps to reopen the club. But his hopes of returning the course to its former glory were dashed when the Taliban seized control of

Kabul in 1996 and at once introduced their brand of hardline Islam. It turned out the mullahs didn't like golf any more than the Communists. They told Afzal that the game came from Shaitan, or the devil – and threw him back in prison.

"In all those years, I never lost my passion for golf," Afzal later confided. "The thought of standing here on the first tee with a club in my hand is what kept me alive."

Succour arrived in 2001 after UN forces ousted the Taliban and placed an interim coalition government in power. Since then golf has returned to Kabul, although the course is still essentially a battle site. There is still no running water. Fairways are scrubland and greens are black circles rolled from diesel and sand.

Yet eighteen red flags wave defiantly in the ever-present wind. The course has been swept for mines and Afzal further reassures the occasional guests that he still has both legs despite walking every inch of the course. It will take $200,000 to restore the course to its seventies heyday, but for now Afzal is more than happy to have a tolerant government in place and a golf club open and ready for play.

"My friends used to tell me I looked like an old man," he says. "Now, since the course reopened, they tell me I look like a young boy in love."

Here we have a golfer with the bravery to play and pratice in the knowledge that, if seen, he would be tortured and possibly even killed. We have a prisoner-of-war, locked in solitary confinement for eighteen months, who saved his sanity by playing mentally in his cell. And can you imagine coming back from a near-fatal injury – one that costs you an arm and a leg – to become a golfing champion, playing off a scratch handicap? We'd label it impossible if it hadn't actually been accomplished.

It is the ultimate accolade to the game of golf that it can be used in harrowing circumstances like these to foster such positive and profound results. But of course, these achievements would not have been possible were it not for the extreme bravery of each story's hero. And while we might never find ourselves in their positions, their stories might just help us put that pressure we feel over a short putt into some sort of perspective.

7

The Club that Swings Itself

Some of the more bizarre journeys to the edge of golf can be found in the sphere of the game's equipment, and the barmy army of bemused and brilliant inventors who populate it. In what other sport, for example, might you get a ball whose core was made out of a bull's penis? A tobacconist called Mr Walter Langstaff – if that is indeed his real name – patented this notion back in 1912. His argument was that by using "a resilient animal substance which at present is more or less a waste product of the slaughterhouse," you could make a ball that was at once durable and cheap. But despite stumbling across the ultimate cock-and-bull story, Langstaff was destined for obscurity; let's be nice and put the failure of his grand idea down to the advent of the popular Haskell ball, invented just ten years earlier.

Langstaff's ball is typical of a subculture of bizarre golfing inventions, and the quirkiness is an apposite comment on the world's desperation to improve. Golf is officially a Very Tough Game, and the vast majority of the world's 60 million players have no trouble getting that message across. The desire – the need – to get better is present in almost all of us. We will try pretty much anything that might shave a couple of shots off our score – although we evidently draw the line at teeing up a bull's privates.

This mania has seen creative minds applied to golf like no other game. Some are interested because of the potential for profit from a helpful creation; others have a more philanthropic motivation, feeling the need to help release us from our suffering. But one thing they have in common is a readiness to try anything.

Ably demonstrating this is golf's best but least-celebrated inventor – a Sussex pensioner named Arthur Paul Pedrick. Pedrick, born in 1912 and sadly no longer with us, spent his entire working life in the examiners' section of the United Kingdom Patents Office. His life revolved around concepts and ideas and he duly spent his retirement bombarding the office he formerly served with 161 patent applications throughout the 1960s and 1970s.

Pedrick's passion for ideas went gloriously unhindered by bothersome complications like common sense and practicality. His suggestions ranged from irrigation of Australia's deserts by using giant peashooters to fire snowballs from Antarctica, to a "Chromatically Selective Cat Flap" that would recognize your cat's color and let it through only. Pedrick's own cat, who crops up time and again in his patent applications, was ginger. Somewhere between the two, Pedrick devised a ladder that would help spiders climb out of the bath.

Mercifully for the world of golf, Pedrick was a weekend hacker. Far more philanthropist than mercenary, he would spend countless hours applying his grey matter to the irritations of the game. "I was frustrated with my slicing and hooking," he said in 1970, "and I spent a lot of time looking for the damn ball in the rough. It was infuriating."

In his efforts, Pedrick was certainly not about to let his imagination be confined by so prosaic a publication as golf's rule-book. Typical of his genius was UK Patent GB1251780, relating to, as Pedrick put it, "A tee which, upon sensing a bad swing of the driver, would, through a puff of air, shoot the golf ball off the tee just before the club hits the ball."

Pedrick described his notion thus: "Such a tee, in combination with a series of light rays and photocell units, linked to a control box which can release pulses of compressed air into the tee, can prevent a ball from being driven at all if it is going to be sliced or hooked badly."

Whether the invention would have worked for clubs other than the driver, we will never know. For like all Pedrick's golfing notions, Patent GB1251780 had no trouble finding its way on to the drawing board but struggled to negotiate any sort of passage off it.

Of similar brilliance and uselessness is patent GB1192139, in which a wooden-headed club's face is fitted with a series of vertical rubber blades. These are designed to offer some resistance to the ball at impact, while bending back. The blades not deformed by impact would stand firm, preventing the ball from rolling across the face – the action that creates sidespin.

Pedrick also had plans for a pool-cue putter and a tee peg that would suspend the ball above it with electrostatic forces. But my personal favorite was his concept of a multi-route golf course with several fairways, designed to cater for the hooker and slicer. "It is far more natural to produce a sliced or hooked drive than a straight hit and this has led to the suggestion that golf courses should be planned with dual fairways," Pedrick reasoned. No arguments here.

But the concept that appears to be most tantalizing for the golfing inventor is a golf ball that flies straight however horribly you hit it. The notion crops up time and again over the past century or so, and Pedrick was just one of several designers who spent time and effort on the subject. Predictably, Pedrick's solution is the most outlandish. UK Patent GB1121630 saw him striving to control the spin on a golf ball by adding a series of flaps to its surface. These flaps, he argued, would in normal circumstances be held flush to the ball's cover by magnets. If the golfer miscues and applies enough sidespin to the ball, the centrifugal force created by the spin overcomes the power of the magnets, and the flaps spring up to calm the hook or slice.

"If this can be achieved," wrote Pedrick grandly in his patent application, "considerable benefits will have been added to the general happiness of the human race, or at least to those members of the "species" addicted to the game of golf."

Back in the 1950s one Professor Sinnatt MC, BSc, Fellow of Royal Aeronautical Society, designed a self-correcting gyroscopic golf ball. However much you hooked or sliced it, it would fly straight. He approached the North British Rubber Company with a view to production, but this was back in the days when businessmen had ethics, and they turned him down on the grounds that such a ball would not be good for golf.

Then again, in the late 1970s another self-correcting ball was invented – and this time manufactured. Called the Polara, the ball, launched in 1977, was designed by two non-golfers; an IBM chemist named David Napala and a physicist at San Jose State University named Fred Holmstrom. The two men achieved its arrow-like flight from an asymmetrical dimple pattern. The ball had six rows of normal-size dimples around its equator, but elsewhere was covered in very shallow dimples. This caused the ball to adjust its spin axis midflight in a way that toned down sidespin. When America's ruling body, the

United States Golf Association, banned the ball on the grounds that it would "reduce the skill required to play golf," Napala and Holmstrom sued – eventually winning $1.375 million in an out-of-court settlement. They did, though, have to agree to withdraw the ball.

The Polara, though, has made one U-turn. It is back in golf now as a strictly recreational-play ball, after American company Pounce Sports acquired the rights for the ball from the U.S. copyright office.

"We want to give players like ourselves a chance to better enjoy a great game," says Pounce Sports general manager Andy Gesek. "This is not about winning a club championship." Pounce reckon the Polara is 75 percent straighter than standard symmetrical balls; effusive testimonies from their customers appear to corroborate that outlandish claim.

Then again, at the end of the millennium, another gyroscopic ball turned up. This one was designed by Chicago-based physicist and amateur golfer Tom Chapman. And the tale of Chapman's creation offers real insight into the workings of the golf inventor's mind.

"I guess I am known as an expert regarding gyroscopes," Chapman avers modestly. "So I tend to see situations where gyroscopic effects either exist or could exist.

"One day, maybe fifteen years ago, I learned that a wedge shot often had a backspin speed of 12,000rpm, and I remember commenting that that was not much slower than a dentist's drill. Shortly after, it dawned on me that if the golf ball had a vertical structure inside, like a rubber doughnut, of slightly greater density than the rest of the core, such a fast-spinning ball would actually be a gyroscope, with all the effects that includes."

A gyroscope is fundamentally a device for maintaining direction. It works through a principle known as conservation of angular momentum – a spinning device resists changes to its movement as a result of the axis and momentum of its spin. The more the gyroscope's rotor rotates, the more it resists deflections to its path.

"Imagine a golf ball with a doughnut-shaped weight inside it, so that when the ball is on the tee, the doughnut is standing on edge, with the plane of the doughnut carefully lined up with the flag," Chapman expands. "Once the golf ball is struck, the high-speed backspin makes this doughnut spin rapidly backwards, exactly like a gyroscope. The axis of the spinning ball cannot help but remain constant during flight. No sidespin can occur."

Chapman, who has a college degree in nuclear physics from the University of Chicago, conducted his first experiments with nothing more exotic than a batch of elastic bands. "I did not want to invest massive money to check it out, so I simply took half-a-dozen plastic practice balls and wrapped standard very thick rubber bands around them. I sat them on the tee so that the bands aligned vertically; this, of course, was not that easy."

Chapman proceeded to hit the balls at a narrow tree trunk that was around ten yards away. "I found that with standard practice balls, I could actually hit the tree about one time in every ten tries. When I did the same with the practice balls with the rubber bands around them, I could hit the tree around six times out of ten. I interpreted that as an accuracy that was around six times as good."

The results encouraged Chapman to experiment with regular golf balls, complete with that denser, doughnut-shaped rubber object inside to give the ball its spinning axis – and this is where his plan hit a snag. There are not many companies who manufacture golf balls, and those that do quoted him enormous amounts of money to create prototypes.

"Eventually it dawned on me that I could drill a precise pattern of holes around the ball's diameter, in which I could then insert brass screws," Chapman continues. "The brass is more dense than the ball, so they would duplicate the effect of a rubber torus (doughnut) inside."

When Chapman started hitting these screw-filled balls, he could not believe his eyes. "Every time I hit one of those balls, I always wound up laughing because of how ridiculously straight they always flew. Only cross-winds ever affected it, and even that was minimal.

"But the funniest part was when one landed on a side slope. Obviously golf balls kick sideways when they hit, and often end up in bad places. But the gyroscopic golf ball even bounced straight. The spin of the ball essentially would not let the ball get kicked sideways, even off steep side slopes. It was the funniest thing I ever saw."

The concept of the self-correcting golf ball is a paradoxical notion to a golfer. At first it sounds fantastic, but at some stage the thought dawns on you that it's a bit like giving a 100-meter sprinter a motorbike instead of a set of blocks. An auto-straight golf ball neatly extracts any sense of achievement out of hitting an accurate shot; but this is not something that especially bothers Chapman.

"There are two sorts of golfers," he insists. "Fewer than five percent seem to really accurately know where the ball is going to go. The rest, including me, hit and hope. This larger group includes massive numbers of "duffers." If golfers consider it acceptable to take Mulligans (a free second chance after a poor tee shot), that suggests to me that they would like to get better scores than they are normally capable of. I have a suspicion that there are many duffers that would want balls that flew straight so that they looked less incompetent to their friends."

Despite the positive, demonstrable success of Chapman's experiments, he has so far failed to get the ball to market. Part of this might be the fact that the ball would fail the USGA's symmetry rule, enforced in the wake of "Polaragate" in 1980. The law stipulates that a ball should essentially perform the same, regardless of where on the ball's surface it is struck or how it is oriented on the tee. Chapman's GyroBall manifestly does not.

A related drawback is that the ball cannot be used anywhere other than the tee shot. "The ball cannot be hit for the second stroke, because its equator is invariably lying at some bad angle," Chapman concedes. "If it is hit then, it does all sorts of strange things, like sometimes wobbling in flight, or bouncing really strangely. Putting with it is especially funny. So if my ball were used on a drive, it always needs to be replaced with a conventional ball for all the rest of the strokes.

"I consider the GyroBall to be sort of a "novelty," where if it were ever manufactured, only duffers would buy them for recreational purposes."

It is perhaps surprising that such an apparently mundane object as a small ball can inspire so much left-field thinking. Yet the list goes on. Someone has even managed to invent a square one, although to be fair to its creator, Scottish scientist Eric Farr, his cube ball, heavily weighted with sand or water – was always intended to be nothing more than a practice device to build power.

Six years before Mr Langstaff was coming up with his bull's-pizzle ball, tire and rubber manufacturer Goodrich introduced a ball with a rubber core filled with compressed air. Called the

"Pneu-matic," the ball's liveliness gave it some early popularity. Its allure started to fade, however, when golfers discovered it had a tendency to explode in hot weather. Rumors began to circulate of unfortunate souls who had suffered the blast while warming the ball in their trouser pockets. Unfortunately for Goodrich, this is the type of hearsay that doesn't need to be true to have a disastrous effect on sales.

Meanwhile, inventors have excelled themselves in coming up with solutions for one of the game's more frustrating and expensive problems: the lost ball. Arthur Pedrick himself suggested that a ball's innards should have the ability to reflect radio waves. The golfer, carrying a simple homing device, would therefore be able to locate his ball in the rough – though, had his special cover flaps worked in the first place, it presumably would not have ended up there.

Relying rather less on physics and more on faith is the Golfinder, effectively a dowsing rod that asks its users to wander through the woods divining for golf balls. "Hold our antenna against the side of your torso," they advise, "and walk in the general area of your lost golf ball until your Golfinder picks up the signal. Presto. The compass arm points to the hidden ball."

When it comes to how it works Golfinder are, like their product, keeping things close to their chest. "It uses your native energy," is all they are prepared to give away. "Please don't ask us for the theory of its operation. That's our business and the main reason we haven't applied for patents – which would expose the technology."

More understandable but just as baffling is the worryingly titled Never-Lose-Another-Golf-Ball Putter, designed by American company Hammacher Schlemmer. The company has a history of innovation – they were one of the first to sell car-repair kits in New York, while also laying claim to introducing the pop-up toaster back in 1930. But the Never-Lose-Another-Golf-Ball putter is, shall we say, rather more niche.

The product is a normal putter fitted with a spin-cast fishing reel halfway up the shaft. The fishing line runs down the shaft and is attached to a normal golf ball. The idea is to hit the putt, then reel in the ball. Hammacher Schlemmer insist the line is too thin to affect the roll of the ball – but cannot name three people who have ever lost a ball on a putting green.

And what of the golf club itself? Genuinely radical designs do not crop up that often; ever-tighter rules governing club construction have tended to limit new designs to subtle rephrasing of old ones. But thankfully there are still enough inventors out there with the vision, courage and imagination to present the world of golf with something truly different. And while golf-ball inventions tend to be based around hitting straighter, the recurring theme for club design is hitting it further.

In 1978, Oregon's George Greer announced plans for a driver where the ball would literally explode off the clubface. His plan was to construct a club with an inbuilt explosive charge that would detonate as club impacted with ball.

This notion, in fact, was not new; people had been experimenting with clubhead explosives for decades. But Greer believed they had been going about it the wrong way – literally. Previous devices had typically included a mechanism for pushing a ball away from the clubhead at the moment of impact; Greer believed they were destined to fail because the recoil created by the explosion caused the club to slow down.

Greer's notion was to turn the explosive mechanism around so that the charge detonated *away* from the ball (and the target) rather than behind it. His club would feature a barrel running right through the head, complete with a rear-facing muzzle. The barrel would be loaded with what was effectively a shotgun cartridge. The cartridge, though, would not be full of pellets; it would explode through a rapidly expanding gas cylinder. In his patent application Greer described its operation thus:

> The golfer will perform his normal driving swing. If the swing is straight and true, the ball will contact the outer portion of the firing pin. This will drive the inner portion of the pin against the primer cap which will explode and detonate the propellant charge. Upon detonation the propellant charge will be converted into hot gasses which will be discharged through the muzzle of the barrel.
>
> The discharge of gasses from the cartridge will accelerate the clubhead toward the ball, imparting additional energy to the ball and extending the distance to which it is driven.

And what if the swing was not straight and true? The ball misses the firing pin, and the detonation cannot take place. Greer saw this as a good thing; the inevitable poor shot created by the wonky swing would not receive a big enough boost to hurtle the ball out-of-bounds.

The concept of the exploding clubhead surely reached its apogee in 1996, with the invention of the golf club you don't even need to swing. The Swingless Golf Club, invented by Californians Roy Taylor and James Duncalf, has a piston in its head, which explodes forwards a few inches at 180mph thanks to the detonation of a plastic strip of five powder charges, punching out into the back of the ball. You simply sit the clubhead an inch behind the ball and pull the trigger. The piston, which has a lofted front to send the ball airborne, can fire the ball anywhere from 25 to 200 yards thanks to a range-adjustment facility.

Duncalf and Taylor's first prototype used a firing system from a .22-caliber rifle. "We just attached it to the club we'd made, so you'd just pull the trigger and it would go off," Duncalf recalls. Happily, safety was never far from their thoughts. They had originally planned to use a six-round rotating cartridge but gave up on the idea when they realized it would allow the player to carry a live round without realizing it. In the final design, the .22 cartridges come four in a pack. The pack must be rotated manually after each shot.

The club also features an orientation sensor in its grip that stops the club going off in any position other than its playing position, and in addition the trigger has a safety latch.

Naturally the club is not legal, not that it was ever submitted to the USGA for approval. Instead, Taylor and Duncalf were targeting those folks who wanted to play but lacked the fitness, athleticism or ability to swing the club. "There are millions of golfers in this country and they are becoming an aging group," says Duncalf. "When golfers get over fifty-five, something between a third to half of them become unable to make the long drives." Swingless Golf also believe the club that swings itself would be ideal for those with back problems, or even non-playing spouses who want to join their partner for a round.

1998 saw Texans Ajay Joshi and Kurt Marshek make their own contribution to club power. In May they filed for a patent for a jet-propelled golf club. Their idea was to build a club with a hollow shaft. The grip end of the shaft was to be attached to a pump system, which could force fluid down the shaft at high pressure. The water would exit via tiny holes in the back of the clubhead, adding forward thrust to the club. The golfer would be able to control the pump, thereby timing the injection of high-pressure fluid to the clubhead. There would even be a flow valve, allowing the golfer to set the amount of thrust needed for the shot.

According to Joshi and Marshek's patent application, the jet-propulsion system urges the "golf club to swing faster, impelling the golf ball farther down the golf course and/or teaching the golfer to swing faster." The patent was granted in October 1999. But despite the undoubted genius in the concept, the jet-propelled golf club has failed to turn its creators into household names.

Maybe not a million miles away was Manchester-based inventor Leonard Challenor's "Whistling Club." Patented in 1936, this again had holes in the clubhead – although this time, they were to allow air through. Here was Challenor's theory: "Air, on entering and passing through the holes during the making of the stroke, will tend to keep the club straight, or straighten any tendency to leave the direct line, so that the moment it reaches the ball it will be in the position it was placed when addressing the ball." The golfing world remains waiting to see this proved. Challenor added: "A further instructive feature is that the passage of air through the holes will produce a distinctive sound, which may assist the player to correct an error in the stroke." Unfortunately, although the concept of noise-related feedback is something that has cropped up in training aids in recent years, the whistling club hit something of a bum note.

Rejection is an occupational habit for golfing inventors. They must develop resilience, and GyroBall inventor Tom Chapman is the perfect example. The lack of movement on his ball did not dissuade him from pursuing other golf-related projects, one of which is the GyroClub, in which a small, motorized gyroscope is placed on the shaft of the golf club, up near the grip end.

"The main characteristic of a gyroscope is that it wants to keep the direction of the axis of rotation constant," Chapman explains. "That could be beneficial to a golfer in terms of swing plane, a vital part of golf-swing technique. The gyroscope must be mounted at a certain very specific angle, so that the rotating weight of the gyroscope will spin in the desired plane of the golf swing. Then, when you make your action, any deviation from that plane is flagged up by the resisting effect of the gyroscope. I really suspect that the majority of golfers, even pros, could benefit from it."

Unfortunately, that is not yet a view shared by any manufacturer. Indeed, Chapman joins Challenor, Pedrick, Joshi, Marshek and the rest in Anonymityville. Sadly, the cream of golf-innovations' creative minds appear destined to live their lives in obscurity.

Even on the rare occasions when their inventions do find their way into mainstream production, they are usually forced to look on while others steal the limelight for their great creations. New Jersey dentist William Lowell is often credited with the 1922 "birth" of the tee peg, helped as he was by a publicity campaign that included advertising with Walter Hagen. Fully thirty years earlier, though, Surrey unknown Percy Ellis was producing a pegged tee known as "Perfectum."

And while most people credit Gene Sarazen with the genesis of the sand wedge in 1931, it was in fact invented by a Texan named Edwin Kerr MacClain. MacClain's sand wedge, patented in 1928, featured what was called an "extended bottom wing" and a concave face. The club was quickly made illegal, but not before Bobby Jones used one to win the Open Championship in

1930.

It's even happened in recent times. Gary Adams, founder of gear company Taylor Made, is widely regarded as the father of the modern metal wood; the club, though, was originally designed in the mid-seventies by a nuclear physicist non-golfer named John Zebelean, who couldn't understand why wood, comparatively inefficient at transferring energy, was used to make golf's power clubs.

Inventing golf equipment may be one of golf's more unsung jobs, but it is far from its most boring. The golf industry has its share of dull occupations; how would you like to spend your days selling tee pegs or cleaning mucky golf shoes? But the characters in the next chapter prove that if you look hard enough, you can find some incredible ways to make your living out of the game.

Burial Service – Course Closed

When I was a teenager, learning the game, I dreamed of becoming a golf professional. Of course, there is nothing unusual about that – except that I did actually manage it. OK, maybe it wasn't the glamorous globetrotting, fortune-amassing, household-name type of pro. I was more of the pro-shop-inhabiting, 70-hour-week-working, chocolate-bar-selling, pittance-earning type. I spent three years doing this before giving it up as a bad job. Still, I suppose my dream came true – albeit in a rather more literal way than I had in mind.

Despite this chastening experience, the notion of earning a living from the game I love still appealed to me – as it does to all golfers from time to time. And many folks manage it. From Tiger Woods to the man who cleans the toilets at the local municipal course, golf creates a livelihood for hundreds of thousands of people, most of whom jump at the opportunity to make cash without having to leave their favorite environment. Most of these jobs are familiar to us – the tour pro, the green keeper, the caddie, the clubhouse caterer – but from time to time the game's many dimensions throw up some wonderfully curious roles. We start with a green keeper whose primary task is to reach the end of the day without being eaten.

Henry Venter is on to the ninth green at Skukuza Golf Club, lining up his first putt, when he hears some sudden loud splashing noises. Looking up, he is met by the irksome sight of two hippos bearing down on him. Fortunately they are more interested in each other than him; these are two males, fighting over territory, and they have selected the green as an appropriate battleground. Venter and his playing partners retreat to the edge of the putting surface to watch the bout, which lasts for fifteen minutes. Eventually a panting victor and vanquished slope back off to the lake, and Venter can return to his putt – which, as you may have guessed, now requires a new line.

The nine-hole Skukuza is the only golf course within the boundaries of South Africa's Kruger National Park, wildlife haven and home to the African "big five" of lion, leopard, buffalo, elephant and rhino. The course has no fences or boundaries; tending its fairways and greens is therefore one of golf's more varied and challenging jobs.

But it's one Venter, a 54-year-old South African and 11-handicapper, accepts with relish – and he is not as distraught as you might think at the sight of two hippos wreaking havoc on one of his greens. "Sure, hippos are quite heavy," he understates. "But in fact they don't do too much damage. They can walk across the green and leave it unmarked. Running is bad though, and fights are obviously not good. But even then we are able to repair the damage with nothing more exotic than pitch-mark repairers."

This is just as well; hippo wars happen four or five times a month at Skukuza. "It happens pretty much whenever one male comes into another's territory," Venter says. "We built a man-made lake to irrigate the course, and now there are forty-eight hippos living in it. There are plenty of crocodiles too. It is called Lake Panic, probably named after the experience of building it."

In fact Venter's most persistent headaches are caused by warthogs, which use their tusks to forage for termites in the fairways and tees. "They are here all the time," he says. "Even today there were seven piglets and two mummies on the sixth fairway. There are too many to count. They burrow big pot-holes up to six inches deep. There's nothing to be done about it; we're in the park here and they can do what they want. But fortunately they do not damage the greens; the spray we use means there are no termites for them there."

The warthogs are the reason you will no longer find any sand bunkers at Skukuza – after any kind of rain the hogs would jump down into the traps and thrash about, effectively trashing the hazard. "Give a warthog a mix of sand, mud and water, and you have a happy warthog," adds Venter.

Skukuza is a pretty parkland-style course with eighteen tees to its nine greens and plenty of trees – although these again keep Venter busy. "In the dry season, when the course is still green, the elephants come on to the golf course. They constantly damage the trees, pushing them over while stripping them for food. They probably take out around sixty-five trees a year, so we rehabilitate and plant new ones."

Venter has one other constant problem to deal with – urine and faeces. "In fact on one Sunday morning I got to the course at ten o'clock. And there, on the ninth green, were two guys putting out between two immense buffalo turds. I toyed with removing it myself, but in the end I sent off one of the caddies to do it.

"Unless instantly removed, animal waste burns the grass. If a giraffe pees in the night, by morning it is too late. The grass dies, but in fact it then grows back greener. We've learned simply to take nature's course to recovery."

Venter gets to play a few holes each week, if he is lucky. And as well as keeping the course in top condition, he also plays a major role in keeping it safe. The course is open on all sides and all of the Kruger Park's wildlife is free to come and go as it pleases. Visitors must ultimately take responsibility for their own safety – all players sign an indemnity form before playing – and although (miraculously) there are no records of anyone being so much as injured at Skukuza, playing here is by definition unpredictable. Just recently a group of Germans stood rooted to the spot on the third hole while five lions swaggered past them, fifteen yards away.

Venter's day begins at 5.30 a.m. "I will head out around the course to see what is around, and what has happened during the night. Last Saturday we found a dead buffalo – a lion kill – on the fourth fairway, with the lions still feasting on it. I could not get the lions to leave, so I had to phone for a helicopter. We had to wait for the chopper to arrive and chase the lions away before we could begin play."

Throughout the day there are people working on the course, and they report anything they see to Venter. "Most animals I can deal with – elephants, for example, will tend to move off if you clap your hands and make a noise. If I can't, I might enlist the help of a park ranger. They can get here within five or ten minutes."

On arrival golfers are given some written matter on what to do if they see anything, and the advice tends to amount to "Back Away Slowly." "People always ask about lions, but actually they aren't that bad," insists Venter. "As those Germans discovered, you can stand there and they will walk past. Leopards on the other hand are more aggressive. You might not see them as often but they are around. Do not look into their eyes. If you make eye-contact with one, watch out."

One regular visitor who has never caused any grief is Golf Ball, an old giraffe, so-called because of an odd white knob on his forehead. "He's a very peaceful old guy," says Venter. "On one occasion I hit a ball which ran up between his legs. I wouldn't recommend visitors to do it, but I just walked up to the ball and putted it out. He wasn't bothered; he just watched me."

Putting out between a giraffe's legs is one of many amazing experiences Venter enjoys while performing his duties at Skukuza. Every four months he gets to watch 200 buffalo swarm across the course on their way to Lake Panic. And as we speak, he gazes out to a series of sunset-bathed fairways on which 300 impala and their young are grazing.

"It's so fantastic to see these sights and have these experiences," he concludes. "Animals come first here and the course adapts to their rhythms; there's a terrific feeling of going with the flow. Looking after a course like this might be a handful, but I can think of worse ways to earn a living."

So can I – sitting in a draughty pro-shop for seventy hours a week for a start. Another would surely be working in a mortuary . . . but then again, perhaps not. If you have ever wondered what a funeral parlor has in its basement, you probably thought along the lines of corpses, caskets and coffins. If, on the other hand, you were thinking "a golf course," there are two possibilities; either you need help, or you have heard of Ahlgrim and Sons Funeral Parlor in Palatine, Chicago.

For, below the parlor's chapel, where 300 burial services take place every year, there is a nine-hole miniature golf course. And yes, it has a haunted-house theme, complete with skulls, scary soundtracks, snakes, spiders, guillotines and gravestones.

The course was built by the parlor's owner, Roger Ahlgrim, back in 1964. "I'm not a proper golfer; I'll play once a year on a full-size course," he says. "But I've always adored miniature golf. We moved here in the sixties, and we had this big basement which we were going to use for future chapels. But at the time our activity didn't warrant it. I had time on my hands, and we had three kids coming up. So I decided to build a miniature golf course for them, and their friends. Maybe a little bit for me too."

The course was finished in 1965 but, like Augusta National, home of the Masters, it gets tinkered with every year. "I'm always making little upgrades and additions," Ahlgrim says, and the current layout – surrounded by slithering synthetic serpents – is certainly worthy of a hole-by-hole look. Roger Ahlgrim talks you through his creations:

> 1st hole: "The main feature here is a sand trap that you have to hit over. But sitting in the sand, staring you in the eye, is a skull; not a real one, but a metal one that I acquired from mortuary school."
>
> 2nd: "These days, if we want to move bodies around the country we do it by air. But back in the seventies we would send them by rail. The body and casket would be put in special shipping containers. On the second hole you putt down one of these, an actual one that was used a few decades ago. There are several holes at the end, and once your ball disappears into those their tunnels crisscross, out of sight, so your ball doesn't come out where you think."

3rd: "The main feature here is a guillotine. You have to get the ball through before the blade chops down. Get this wrong and you'll set off some scary music."

4th: "This hole has a pinball theme; your ball pings about among a series of headstones, before coming down a ramp back to the hole."

5th: "This one's the windmill hole. In fact there's nothing scary here; the sails are not lopping anyone's head off or anything like that. Every miniature course has a windmill hole. Plus my mother's family is from Holland. In fact, we even have a huge windmill, about one-fifth scale, in the car park here. So we put this hole in for her."

6th: "There is a haunted-house theme here. Your ball goes up a ramp into a brown wooden house, which has skulls looking out at you through the window. There are plenty of spiders, and a series of dismembered hands crawling out of the chimney."

7th: "My daughter-in-law built me a mausoleum for this hole. You putt the ball into it, and there are three areas where it can come out. If it bounces into the graveyard, it's a one-shot penalty, but if it bounces into an open grave – there are three of them – it's an extra-shot penalty. If you get lucky, you avoid both."

8th: "This one has a lighthouse theme. It's not too scary, although there is a snake on top of the lighthouse."

9th: "A fairly friendly end here, where your ball runs up a ramp and then down past a running waterfall. Oh yes, and a coffin."

Ahlgrim's incredible course is the centerpiece of a basement containing other entertainments including a shuffleboard course, ping-pong, video games and bumper pool. The place is open to everyone, and it is completely free. "We've never advertised it," he says. "But it gets incredibly busy. We could have groups in every night. We have groups of Cub Scouts, Brownies, YMCA, families stage birthday parties here . . . but it's not all kids. We recently hosted the local Homeowners' Association, and our fire department had their Christmas party here."

The course, though, has to shut down when the funeral parlor is conducting a service. "We have to cancel if we have business," insists Ahlgrim. "It would be disrespectful. Sometimes at the wakes, people ask if the children they have brought along can go down and play, but again we can't do that. The noise comes up through the heating duct in the chapel; we can't very well conduct a burial service to the soundtrack of scary haunted-house music coming up from below."

But of course the inevitable has happened; Ahlgrim has heard the telltale sounds of people playing the course while he is conducting a service. "The trouble is our supply room is down there too, so we don't always have the door locked," he laments. "Then suddenly we hear the noises, the balls rattling about. So far it's never been too bad. I think my ears are more tuned in to those sounds."

At first, Ahlgrim was worried the locals would find his macabre course a tad distasteful. But his fears were, aptly for his line of work, swiftly laid to rest. "My daughter would have sleepovers with her friends, and they would set up in sleeping bags in the lounge, just next door to the basement of a funeral home. But the parents never thought it was a problem," he recalls. "And now, we get people making arrangements for their parents who have passed away, and they will tell us, "I was here twenty years ago playing miniature golf in the basement – do you still have it?" They feel they can come back, so thankfully, it hasn't put them off. In fact I think it's helped them feel at ease with our set-up here."

So while Ahlgrim does not exactly make a living out of the course, it appears to have done his business no harm. And it has made working in a funeral parlor a little more, shall we say, lively. Roger Ahlgrim himself is reckoned to be the man to beat around his own course – "I get the most practice," he adds modestly – and is the course record holder, though he doesn't know what it is.

Ahlgrim also insists the course is not haunted. "I guess haunted houses are where people have died, and no one actually dies here," he suggests. "In fact, I'll probably be the first! Perhaps I'll come back and haunt my course – now that would create the ultimate haunted-house mini-golf challenge."

Over the years, several people have tried to make a buck out of linking golf with music. It's normally hit a bum note. The official line on 1969 Open Champion Tony Jacklin's career was that it went sharply downhill after Lee Trevino chipped in against him three times to claim the 1972 Open. In reality the album he released the same year – *Tony Jacklin Swings* – may have had more to do with it. "The highlight was my rendition of 'Come Fly With Me,'" Jacklin divulged years later, to widespread surprise; the world had come to the conclusion that the album didn't have a highlight. "I thought I did well," added Jacklin, "yet somehow I never overtook the Beatles in popularity."

Elsewhere, golf songs have been largely limited to corny token offerings with such titles as "Let's Play A Round," or "We All Wind Up In A Hole." The vaguely hummable "Straight Down The Middle," as crooned by Bing Crosby, is the nearest we have come to an exception.

When it comes to penning a successful musical, there do not appear to be any hard-and-fast rules on the subject matter. Who would have thought a flying nanny, a bunch of felines, a reclusive wizard and a singing nun would prove so popular? But there is, evidently, one unspoken mandate – don't touch sport. So when New York theater impresario Eric Krebs approached songwriter Michael Roberts about putting together a musical on golf, his response was along the lines of, "You must be crazy."

"There was no precedent for it," Roberts explains. "Plus my read on the worlds of theater and sport – both of which I love individually – is that they've never been successful when put together. It's just not the same audience; theatergoers and golfers are not usually the same people. Certainly in the States, sport tends to be played more by the men while theater tickets tend to be bought by the women; the men go grudgingly."

But Krebs would not let it lie. "I just felt there was something in this," he says. "I did some research and discovered that there are thirty-five million golfers in the U.S. – and no golf musical for them. In some ways it was a commercial decision, but I also had the notion that it could end up being quite funny."

So Krebs asked Roberts to write a couple of numbers about golf. "I wrote two songs," continues Roberts. "Eric heard them and said, "Great, now write sixteen more." He wanted a show of eighteen songs. I told him I couldn't, that there weren't eighteen songs about golf. In the end I took the game up again for inspiration – I hadn't played since I was a kid. I had lessons and interviewed players, asking them why they played and what they loved about the game. I felt that if the show was to succeed it must be palatable for sports people – if those men were going grudgingly, I wanted to make sure there was something they would actually enjoy when they got there."

From his research, Roberts ended up writing more than thirty songs. After a filtering process with Krebs and a lot of hard work, *Golf: the Musical* debuted off-Broadway in New York in 2003. Partly satirical, occasionally political, never serious, the show has outstripped all expectation and is still playing across the States four years later.

Included in the running order are songs about Tiger Woods, golf widows, playing off scratch, bringing golf to the Gulf, even sexism and racism. But one of the most popular numbers is called "Big Bertha."

In his conversations with golfers, Roberts discovered the subject of equipment dominated. "When I took up the game again, I instantly found myself lusting for a set of Ping irons and a Callaway Big Bertha driver," he recalls. "I discovered I was not alone. I realized most golfers have an almost a fetish-like appreciation for the gear."

Out of this arose the show stopper "Big Bertha," a mock ballad apparently about a man's love for his partner, but in fact about a man's lust for his driver. It begins:

> That style, that face, my arms interlaced around you,
> To hold you is a treat, my life is complete now I've found
>   you,
> Now you are with me, now I only see glorious times
>   ahead,
> Together me and you, there's nothing we can't do, our
> future is unlimited.

The song gets more extreme. "People always like it," says Roberts. "It goes over the top, implying making love to the club – but that's what comedy does, taking something logical and going too far with it."

Big Bertha, with your grip so sure and your head so large,
Big Bertha, from the first time I saw you in my neighbor's
    garage,
I knew you were the one for me, together we'll make
    history,
Big Bertha, you're wortha million bucks to me.

Big Bertha, you're so strong and sleekly styled,
Big Bertha, I want you to have my child,
There's so much club to hit the ball,
I guess size matters after all.

"Big Bertha" is a rare slow number in a lively, upbeat show that lasts two hours. The songs are belted out by The Capital Steps, a satirical, musical-revue group from Washington DC consisting of five actors and one musician. "This is a musical revue," adds Roberts. "I found myself going naturally toward upbeat numbers. I did try writing a couple of serious ones but I hated them. I was asking these men, who might have six a.m. tee times on a Saturday morning, to come out on Friday night, and the last thing I wanted to do was bore them."

A second theme Roberts addressed was the obsessive-compulsiveness of the average golf addict. "When I started talking to people I realized that some folks have a hobby, but golf is infinitely more than that. Either you golf or you don't. You know, it gets very cold here in New York in winter, yet there are people queuing up at five a.m. to get a tee time on the public courses, just hoping it doesn't snow so they can play a round.

"I bring this up on the very last song, an up-tempo send-off called 'I'm going golfing tomorrow'. It starts, 'The north wind is blowing it's ten below and snowing, But I'm going golfing tomorrow.'

"That's not far off the truth. It gets more ridiculous, "My wife is in the hospital" and so on . . . but I've even heard stories of that sort of thing happening."

"Tiger Woods" is a vigorous, jumpy gospel number that compares the great man rather favorably with God. "God can do all these marvelous things, but can he clear a pond with a nine-iron from the rough with the rest of the pack one shot behind?" asks Eric Krebs.

"I've been told Tiger has seen it," adds Roberts, "which is embarrassing. We were part of the pre-tournament entertainment at the 2004 Ryder Cup and Tiger was right there, in the front row. But I wasn't there personally, and I'm not sure if that number was played. Anyway we don't make fun of him . . . except to suggest that he is bigger than God."

The show's political slant is seen in two numbers. "Let's Bring Golf To The Gulf" is a skit on golf being an unofficial indicator of American imperialism. "We heard Syria had opened a course," says Roberts. "We're very liberal here in New York, we're not happy about being at war. So this song is a critique of our President."

The second political song is "No Blacks, No Chicks, No Jews." "You can't talk about golf without addressing its social issues," Roberts asserts. "There's no doubt golf has an element of class issue about it, because it's a traditional and an expensive sport. It's exclusive, probably more by sex than by race. You can't play at Augusta National if you are a woman, which is horrific in modern times. We wanted to address that."

Golf: the Musical even includes some audience partici-pation. Toward the end of the show the actors run an impromptu putting competition. Volunteers hit a succession of putts while the rest of the audience is led through a guide to mastering the famously reserved "golf clap." "We describe it as the most flaccid, anemic applause in the world," Roberts says with a smile.

He sees nothing incongruous with the chirpy, upbeat, positive tone of *Golf: the Musical* and the hangdog, haunted expressions of most golfers. "The show is maybe an escape from that downbeat attitude on the course. But in any case I think the game of golf has become a lot less dour. When I came back to the sport I was struck with how radically the game had changed in this respect. Golfers are showing more emotion than they ever used to. Sergio Garcia? People think of him as a pin-up. I think the game has loosened up quite a bit and that's got to be a good thing."

The production has probably come as close as possible to being entertaining for golfers and non-golfers alike. "There is a song called 'My Husband's Playing Around,' which is all about being a golf widow," says Roberts. "Both sides appreciate that. I was just trying to get into the audience's head. But when the choreography and acting are excellent, it's entertaining no matter what you're talking about."

Roberts certainly succeeded in getting into his own head. "When I got back into golf I discovered that it is more than a hobby, more than a sport, more than a lifestyle . . . it is unique in the world of sport and recreation. In fact the game is now ruining my life because I think about it all the time. I've become one of them. Now I want to play all the time. It is better than a drug."

Coaching golf is, of course, one of the game's more recognized occupations – and our perpetual ineptitude at the game suggests it will be for some time. Of the 60 million folks worldwide who play the game today, only fewer than half have ever broken 100 on an eighteen-hole course. But what if your job was to coach the world's worst swinger? With the world's media looking on?

This dubious honor fell to Californian coach Dean Reinmuth in 2005, and it was only fair that it did; for it was Reinmuth himself who came up with the idea of identifying and correcting the world's worst swing, and he instigated the search for its unfortunate owner in the spring of that year.

"Whenever and wherever you go to play golf, you always see unusual swings," Reinmuth observes, somewhat euphemistically. "Every golfer knows someone who makes him think, "How in the world does that guy hit the golf ball? Why is he still playing?" I just thought it would be a fun and interesting task to let the public vote on who they thought had the worst swing, and then see what we could do with it."

Reinmuth was ably qualified for the task. The 55-year-old has been in golf all his life, first as a caddie, then as an international tournament professional and now, and for the last 29 years, as a coach. In that time he has taught everyone from presidents to pros, with Gerald Ford and Phil Mickelson two of his more famous clients. He has worked with Mickelson since the left-hander was fourteen.

But Reinmuth's confidence was temporarily shaken by the quantity of horrific swings sent in to him. "I had hooked up with the Golf Channel, *Golf Digest* and AOL, and as soon as the campaign was launched we received thousands of pictures and video clips. Some people nominated themselves; others nominated their friends. Hopefully they still talk to each other."

Reinmuth's first job was to select ten swings that stood out as being impressively awful. "You're looking for a swing that will make people shake their heads in disbelief," he adds. Once he found them, he verified through the local club pros that these actions were genuine. Finally, the ten swings were posted on the Internet for a public vote.

This narrowed it down to the top three; then the public voted again. Ultimately the winner of this ignoble title was revealed – a 37-year-old U.S. Air Force security officer named Brian Weir.

"Brian's swing was . . . um . . . very physical – a violent, thrashy swing," Reinmuth recalls. "He had this most unusual finish where his whole body twisted and torqued around. He always fell off-balance, and could hit some really awful shots."

Weir tended to shoot around the 100 mark. "I try to kill every shot, try to hit it to the other side of the planet," he told *Golf Digest* shortly after being selected. "That mind-set makes me tense and rigid. I could take a million practice swings as smooth as can be, but when I see that little white ball, all bets are off; I'm swinging for the fences."

Apart from the violence, Reinmuth also noticed a poor grip that caused the clubface to fan open as it went back. Weir's elbows chicken-winged, instead of folding neatly back and through, and he had a chronic reverse weight shift, shifting forward on the backswing and back on the way down. Despite all these flaws, Weir was far from a rookie; he had been playing for fifteen years, so had his swing locked into his muscles. Reinmuth would have his work cut out.

Their first lesson, filmed by the Golf Channel, took place in June 2005 and lasted an hour. "At first he didn't hit a ball," says Reinmuth. "He just had to make golf swings holding his position, because he swiveled through the ball so wildly that his feet came off the ground.

"After a bit I let him hit some balls – but with a very slow swing speed. He had an eight-iron, and I told him he had to make a full swing but hit the ball no further than a hundred yards. It was all about simply making a swing and holding the finish. Brian had a very difficult time with this because he just had this constant urge to pound the ball.

"It wasn't working. I had to find a way of making him want to accomplish my goal versus his. Eventually I told him that if he hit it past the hundred-yard flag he would owe me a hundred dollars. It worked. Even doing this for an hour, the changes were dramatic."

This first lesson reflected Reinmuth's theory on why golf is, as a rule, played so badly. "The golf swing is complex," he asserts. "You need to focus on acquiring the skill of making the proper movement before using it to hit the shots you want to hit. Unfortunately, the golfer's tendency is to try to do both at the same time. If your focus is on wind, slopes, bunkers or water, you have no chance of acquiring a skill. If a person's desire to play golf is greater than their desire to develop a skill, they won't get better.

"With Brian, he needed to forget about where the ball was going and home in on the new movements he was trying to master."

Reinmuth also developed a plan for Weir, a step-by-step process that his pupil had to follow. The process began simply with learning how to stay balanced through the swing. "There's an old saying in golf," Reinmuth adds. "You can't fire a cannon from a canoe. Foundations may not be fancy, but they are the key component."

Reinmuth worked on Weir's technique mentally as well as physically. "Brian was very open to learning, but his biggest downside was that he wanted to hit everything hard. Most folks want to hit the ball further, and their mechanism for doing that is to swing at the ball harder. It sounds logical. I had to rewire Brian's brain that physical force does not hit a golf ball a long distance – co-ordinated movement does. You could punch a ball with all your strength, but it's only going to go a few yards. It took a while, but eventually the message got through."

From balance Reinmuth moved on to building a backswing that moved Weir's weight behind the ball, and from there to sequencing his swing to co-ordinate body and club movement. It was a layer-by-layer process; each level had to be accomplished before moving on. And at each new stage they started without a ball, so Weir would focus on the movements and not get drawn into shot results.

During the process Reinmuth told Weir that instead of spending hours praticing between lessons, he should instead work in short bursts. "Constant repetitions in a short time frame deliver the message faster and better," he told Weir. "Even a commercial break is long enough to reinforce the message. In a longer session your brain will get sidetracked, and work on other things."

In all, Weir received six one-hour lessons over three months. And the results were extraordinary. "We were shooting footage for the last lesson and Brian was hitting driver after driver dead straight," remembers Reinmuth. "His consistency was fantastic. The cameraman was amazed, and I was relieved. For me, the whole process was like putting an aeroplane through a stress test. Brian's progress confirmed to me that my principles of developing a player stood up.

"I hope as well that we proved to the world's golfers that there is hope for everyone. If the world's worst swinger can make this kind of progress, anyone can. And that was really the message we were trying to get across."

You could not find four more diverse roles than coach, musical composer, crypt mini-golf course manager and green keeper/gamekeeper, and it's a testimony to golf's wonderful versatility that it can support them. But the one thing that unites these disparate positions is passion: Reinmuth, Roberts, Ahlgrim and Venter are all clearly in love with their unique roles in the game. They are testimony to one of the game's stranger attributes: that you don't have to be actively playing golf for the sport to claim you.

A passion for the game underpins all the golfers in this book; and that is why the final chapter is saved for those whose zeal for the game goes way beyond the ordinary – and reminds us why golf is the greatest game in the world.

9

Around the World in 80 Courses

"The passionate are like men standing on their heads," declared the ancient Greek philosopher Plato. "They see things all the wrong way."

In fairness to Plato, he was arriving at his conclusion almost two millennia before the invention of golf. Had he sampled the heady and exquisite seductions of the game firsthand, he might have found himself able to view the admittedly erratic behavior of the world's most fanatical players in a better light.

One man who certainly wanted to see golfers in a better light was Londoner and passionate player William Willett, the man behind daylight-saving time – or British Summer Time. There is a misconception that daylight saving was invented to cut down the need for artificial lighting and boost energy efficiency. It wasn't; it was initially dreamed up to allow people more time to play golf in the evenings.

Willett's thirst to play more golf saw him seek to change time itself. He was fed up that valuable daylight hours that could be spent on the links were wasted because they occurred early in the day, when the world was still in bed. His notion to move the time an hour forward – allowing us to get up closer to dawn and so giving longer evenings – was based on creating more valuable recreation time – which for Willett meant golf. Opponents of DST even labeled the extra hour "golf time." Sadly for Willett his plans were not adopted until 1916, primarily as a First World War economy measure – one year after Willett had died.

As we shall see, the peculiar brand of passion golf engenders among its most ardent acolytes is both marvelous and inspirational, as well as largely insane. Take New Yorker Ralph Kennedy. In 1919 he read that the record for the most courses played by an individual stood at 240. He decided to beat it. By 1932 he had played one thousand, by 1940 it was double that and in 1951 he made St. Andrews number three thousand. His final figure is unknown but reputed to be 3,650 – a number that equates to a new course a day, every day, for ten years.

In fact ever since 1567, when Mary Queen of Scots popped out for a quick nine instead of mourning her husband's death, golfers have shown a bamboozling lack of perspective in the lengths they'll go to for a game. Mary's resultant date with the executioner's block not only made her glad she had worked so hard on keeping her head still; it also proved that the passionate golfer, faced with the prospect of being denied a game, is prepared to risk everything to get to the first tee.

Writing in 1975, journalist and broadcaster Alistair Cooke suggested, "It is a wonderful tribute to the game, or to the dottiness of the people who play it, that for some people somewhere there is no such thing as an insurmountable obstacle, an unplayable course, the wrong time of the day, or the year."

And indeed, for golfers of truly extreme passion, stowing the sticks in the loft for five months while winter bites just isn't an option. They see wind-chill and rock-hard fairways not so much reasons to stay indoors, more as icy, dicey hazards that intensify the challenge of the game. But just how are you supposed to hole a putt when the cup has frozen over?

That was just one conundrum facing a golf-mad fourball from Wisconsin, USA. "Up here the golf season starts just after the first part of April," says Ron Stierman, one of the group. "It shuts down around the end of October. We are all crazy about golf and had been used to playing five or six times a week at Idlewild Golf Club, Sturgeon Bay. So as the season drew to a close we resolved to play golf every month through the winter. We started going out occasionally at weekends, hacking away as best we could. We enjoyed it so much it has become every weekend. We would do it during the week after work, but it gets dark at four-thirty."

There are almost no conditions that will keep Ron and the rest of the fourball – Jim Berg, Tony Smith and Paul Whitelaw Gorski – off the course. They once played in temperatures of –4° F with a 20mph wind. Only thick snow keeps them off – a fine dusting presents no problems at all.

Winter golf at Idlewild means playing on a golf course frozen so solid it makes concrete feel like cotton wool. "And you know, you can use it to your advantage," enthuses Stierman. "Three-hundred-yard drives are suddenly not that hard. And we have a pond on the ninth that you normally have to lay up short of. But in January that ice is four-feet thick, so you can just blast away on to it for a shorter approach shot. We often see ice fishermen out in the open water. They look at us as if we are mad to be out there – and we do our best to return the compliment."

But, as you might expect, the list of problems caused by the conditions is longer than the bonuses. Your drives might bound on, but so do your wedges – twenty feet in the air. You must land short and risk a pinball kick. You must also develop a way of securing the club in thick gloves and swinging the club through five layers of clothes. "Plus you've *got* to rotate your balls," insists Stierman. That sounds tricky enough even without the thick gloves on, until he adds: "I have three on the go – one in play and two getting warm in my pocket."

So we have four grown men of sound mind risking hypothermia and frostbite to watch a small white ball ping about aberrantly on the tundra. Even Stierman is slightly at a loss to explain why. "I guess a passion for golf underpins it," he says eventually. "As you get older you get away from team sports – I played baseball till I was forty-eight. But you still want that competition, and golf – especially this winter variety – offers an amazing opportunity to compete. You can be competitive with yourself, against the course, against other people. You are constantly striving to overcome something that won't readily be overcome, if at all. It's trying to win against all odds, and I think there's a part of the human spirit that likes that. For some reason, as the challenge grows, so does my zeal to meet it."

Stierman also believes a big part of the enjoyment of playing in these conditions is the camaraderie between the foursome, which usually manifests itself through humour and banter.

"We like to play competitively and have come up with all kinds of underhand ways to gain the advantage," he states. "A great tactic is to ice your opponent's putter – in other words, pour water on it. When he grabs it from the bag, it freezes against his skin. It normally takes a couple of holes for him to warm the putter up enough to be able to remove his hand without ripping some skin off."

Another dirty trick involves tying deer antlers to your rival's bag. In Wisconsin winter is deer-hunting time, and your opponent must wander the fairways constantly distracted by the risk of being shot at. "In fact, none of us has ever been shot," Stierman adds hastily. "Although once we were on one of the back holes, which are in the woods, and a shotgun goes off within fifty feet of us. We never saw the hunter or what or who he was shooting at. We took gimmes and moved on."

The group's enjoyment of cold-weather golf has led to their forming a group called the Tundra Golf Association. They have also penned a light-hearted guidebook called *Golf on the Tundra,* essential reading for anyone wishing to play winter golf in a cold climate. Among other things, you will learn what the penalty is for developing hypothermia and where to drop should your ball hit a sledder in the head.

Despite the unbridled relish the quartet show for sub-zero golf, other members of Idlewild have not followed suit. "No one else has joined in," says Stierman, disappointed. "I guess it takes a certain mentality to go out and enjoy playing golf in freezing temperatures, and they are probably a bit smarter than us. But we will keep going when it's bitter because we have a passion for golf and we don't want that passion to die. Every time we play we feel like we are stealing a day out of winter."

The one thing that was not a problem for the Frozen Foursome was getting to the golf course in the first place; it was just a short drive. And for most of us, our passion for golf is not put to the test that much in terms of reaching the first tee; maybe a 25-minute drive along smooth roads in air-conditioned comfort. But for Australian Tom Harold, this was not exactly the case; between him and his nearest golf course lay shark-infested seas, jungle, crocodiles and bush fires. But when you've got to play, you've got to play.

Goulburn Island is a remote and tropical Aboriginal community three miles off Australia's north coast. Its nearest golf course is at Darwin, 275 miles away, a statistic of very little comfort to Harold, a self-confessed golf addict and a teacher at the island's elementary school.

"The job was a lot of fun," says 4-handicapper Harold. "Golf was just going to have to dip out for a while." He had his clubs with him, but the only place clear enough for him to belt balls was the island's airstrip – a makeshift stretch of gravel.

"In fact there was another spot, a mud flat," Harold recalls. "But it was infested with thousands of sandflies and mosquitoes. It'd be swish, swing, swing, swish. I couldn't hit more than maybe thirty balls down there, but at least I got my little fix."

But after eight months without a proper game, Harold was starting to get twitchy. The prospect of competing in Darwin GC's club championship, staged over two consecutive weekends, was too much to turn down. So Harold entered and got himself a Saturday tee-off time. He would have liked to fly to Darwin, but the flight times did not tally with his teaching commitments. If he wanted to make his tee time, Harold would have no option but to spend Friday afternoon boating the three miles to the mainland, then motorbiking the remaining 272 to a friend's house in Darwin. He began to make plans for the hellish journey to the course – plans that backfired almost at once.

"I had a 13.5-foot aluminium tinny, a fishing boat," says Harold. "I put my fueled-up bike in the boat on Friday morning, before class. I wanted to make a quick getaway that lunchtime. Now we have big high tides here, twenty feet or so.

The water goes out miles. When I came back at lunchtime the water was 1,300 feet out and there was no boat."

Harold eventually found his boat in the next bay, 325 feet from the water and about the same from the shore. He was forced to drive his car on to the beach, attach the boat's winch to it then tow the boat to higher, harder ground. He tried to relaunch but the sand was too soft. Eventually he drove around to the other side of the island and launched there.

"By the time I got the boat in the water I was ready to call it off," Harold sighs. "It was 91° F, as humid as you like, and I was sweating like a pig."

But his problems were just starting.

It took Harold 25 minutes to steer the boat to a mainland beach so remote there were no inhabitants for 200 miles. "If you broke your leg, you'd stay there," Harold insists. But the tide was out there too, and the silt meant there was no safe place to dock.

"I went as far as I could, but was still 100 feet short of firm ground," says Harold. "I had to get out of the boat and into mud thigh-deep. I had to take the two wood panels off the bottom of the boat, put the bike on the first, then push it on to the second. Then, keeping the boat balanced, I reached back behind to pull the first one forward and push the bike on to that. And so on to the beach. It was comedy capers."

Harold finally got his bike on to a bush track leading from the beach, and stashed a tin of boat fuel he would need for the return crossing. Driving down the track, he almost at once smelled burning. A bush fire was coming his way. "I had to ride through the front of it," he recalls. "It was OK, but I was thinking about my precious can of fuel. Without it, I was stranded; the fire was heading straight toward it."

Harold chugged down the slippery sandy bush track, falling off at regular intervals. He had planned to refuel at an

Aboriginal settlement called Oen Pelli before 5 p.m., when its garage closed. But it was already 6 p.m. and starting to get dark. He had no option but to plough on to the next place, Jabaroo, and hope his bike made it. But Harold was more worried about being eaten.

"Between Oen Pelli and Jabaroo the dirt road crosses a river," he says. "It's like a concrete ford. This is Kakadu National Park. The river is tidal, and hundreds of massive crocodiles live there. When the tide's in, the water can be five feet deep. I was worried I'd have a lot of water to go through with the crocs either side. I got there at dusk and could just make out that, fortunately, the water was only six inches deep. So I got through OK."

Harold's luck held and he made it to Jabaroo, getting to the fuel pumps five minutes before they closed at 8 p.m. Walking in to pay, he was surprised to see the attendant jump at him. "I didn't understand why till I got a drink out of the fridge and saw my reflection. I was covered in black soot from the fire and bits of blood from falling off. I looked scary-ass."

Harold got his fuel but still had 150 miles to go to Darwin – but at least he would now be on a bitumen road. He got to his friend's house around midnight. "Like an idiot I'd asked for an early morning tee-off time," he groans. "I had about four hours' sleep."

The next morning, Harold shrugged off his journey from hell to start incredibly with four straight pars. "I was thinking, "This is all right!" Then I got on the bogey train. I ended up probably about ten-over."

His Sunday round was not much better. After holing out, Harold jumped back on his bike and set back off on the return leg, knowing that he would be doing the same thing all over again next week for the final 36 holes – and this time with no chance of winning.

Harold got back to the coast to find his fuel tank intact – the fire had not reached it. Setting out to sea in the dark, he lost his bearings. He was forced to head out into the darkness and hope the island appeared in front of him. In the blackness Harold's boat hit a coral bommie, scaring the daylights out of him. Fuel was low too. "I thought I was going to run out. And in this strait you just get whizzed away down one way or the other."

Thankfully, the island appeared in the gloom in front of him. And by the time Harold reported for lessons at 9 a.m. on Monday morning, he was already looking forward to the following Saturday's game. In fact, the harrowing weekend never came close to putting Harold off, and became the first of many long-distance treks he would make to Darwin Golf Club. After his stint teaching on Goulburn, he moved back to the mainland but was now 25 miles *further* from the course. His round trip was now 600 miles. His route would take him through winding sandy, rocky and corrugated bush roads, and across numerous rivers, bogs and creeks. Each journey would last six-and-a-half hours, and to cope Harold bought a bigger bike. And on one of these trips, he won the club championship.

"What drove me to do it? I honestly don't know," he admits. "I just love the challenge of controlling the ball, and the thrill of getting it to go where you aim. I love the course, the camaraderie, the beer after the game. I'd have to say I am addicted to golf. Even if I chopped it last week, I can't wait to play the next.

"That first trip was something I was aiming to do. And when things went wrong I just said, "This isn't going to stop me." It was the challenge of trying to do well when it's tough. Ultimately I suppose it's the same challenge golf offers."

Today Harold lives in the Darwin suburbs. If traffic allows, he can get to the course in precisely 51 seconds.

Harold's adventures are truly extraordinary, but then golf is a game replete with acts of passion. Up on Scotland's remote and beautiful north coast at Royal Dornoch Golf Club, a reclusive Scot named Alan Stein used to play 36 holes a day, every day. Including Christmas. On his own. In a kilt. Advancing years mean he now only plays one round a day.

Then there is mad-keen golfing Irishman Ivan Morris, author of the book *Only Golf Spoken Here*. Morris has given up golf just once in his life – for an afternoon – because he had broken his arm. He was playing the next day though, one-handed, with his arm in a cast. Morris also once asked his wife if she would mind having her labor induced so he could play in the Interprovincial Championship at Royal County Down. She relented; he won the event.

Two Englishmen, W R Chamberlain and George New, once played a game of golf that lasted sixteen years. In 1922 they pledged to play every Thursday, indefinitely, with scores accumulating. In all they played 814 rounds, making extensive notes while they went of everything from pin positions to wind direction. It all ended in 1938, when New died. He had won, taking 42,371 shots to Chamberlain's 44,008. Between them they had recorded more than two million match facts.

Golfers often wax lyrical about the beauty of the sport's playing fields, and in extreme cases these backdrops alone can inspire a passion for the game. If you want an idyllic, dreamy landscape, head to Gleneagles in Perthshire; for dramatic cliff-top golf, California's Pebble Beach can't be touched; for stunning forest and heath land, visit Pine Valley in New Jersey; for challenging mountain golf, try Silvertip in the Canadian Rockies; and for sheer parkland beauty Augusta National – a former nursery replete with a legion of blooms – is, for the golfer, an improved version of the Garden of Eden.

Yet players who have a pure, primordial passion for golf do not need magnificent surroundings to throw themselves into the game; they will play with similar gusto in heaven or hell.

The Air Assault Golf Club is on the outskirts of Port Harcourt, Nigeria's second-largest city. The place is so-named because it is owned by the Nigerian air force, and each hole is named after a high-ranking officer. There are two massive bomb craters on the course, but the military are tight-lipped as to how they got there; theories suggest either bombing during the Biafran War of the 1960s, or perhaps some later bomb testing.

At the Air Assault course you'll find a rather different experience to the comforts of the country club; and you will feel it right from parking up. Young boys guard not only cars but also car-parking spaces. The disparity increases as you get out of your car and survey the scene. Running right down one side of the course is Port Harcourt's busiest road. The road reverberates to the beat of a thousand revving engines; traffic is at a constant standstill and your chances of being able to concentrate on your first tee shot are dented by sudden strident horn-tooting. You note that you will also be playing to a gallery – not just the bored masses in the cars, but the thousands of locals who mill up and down the road all day, usually on their way to and from the city-center markets.

It's not just your ears that are under attack: there is also a serious stench to contend with. Not only are a thousand cars and motorbikes belching exhaust fumes across the fairways, but also Port Harcourt is the hub for the Nigerian petroleum industry. The acrid stench of burning oil hangs in the air, so thick you can almost bang your head on it.

Mixing charmlessly into the odor is the reek of rotting rubbish. On the other side of the course to the road is Port Harcourt's largest shantytown. Garbage from here finds its escape in the golf course, and you can reckon on having to drop your ball away from it at some stage during your round.

The clubhouse is dilapidated; there is no lighting and no adornments of any sort. There is a pro shop but you can expect to find only a handful of items in there – a glove, a couple of clubs, maybe a few balls the pro has bought from the caddies.

Next door to the clubhouse is the caddy shack. The Air Assault course has a hundred caddies, most of whom are very efficient players and all of whom spend a great deal of time there. Conditions may be unsophisticated but they still manage to do all their cooking and washing in the caddy shack. There are always clothes hanging off the washing lines, and you can guarantee your chosen bag-carrier will look immaculate.

"The caddies are polite but do not let themselves get pushed around," says member and passionate golfer Roy Donaldson. "Last year the new club captain decided to make the course tougher by growing the rough. The caddies didn't like this because they get blamed for lost balls. They responded by letting the rough grow, then setting fire to it. We were putting out bush fires for three days."

The course itself is a flat, grassland track with a few trees and almost as many sand bunkers. It features greenish tees and fairways and, instead of greens, sand/oil browns. The mixture for the browns is best described as inconsistent. "One is like lightning," confides Donaldson, "then the next is like putting through a bunker. There is no way you can pitch the ball on the brown and expected it to hold."

Playing the course is a very public affair. For a start you are watched by people from the main road and the shantytown, and there are also plenty of people wandering across the course, often carrying baskets of fruit and other market wares. It is best to give your target one extra look before making your swing; chances are someone will be walking across your line twenty yards ahead of you.

Things get even more confusing when you reach the seventh tee. In front of you is the most basic house you can imagine, just a roof supported by four poles. A middle-aged woman lives inside. Golfers often offer her a few pennies as they play though, or a little more if they are playing well.

Port Harcourt is known for having severe rainstorms. "We can get five inches in a few hours," says Donaldson. "In June and July we often play a sixteen-hole course because the third and the fourth are underwater. Often, hot sun follows the rain and we can get two inches of grass growth in a day. It must be a green-keeper's nightmare."

The golf club also has a curious dress code. You must wear proper socks, tailored shorts and a shirt with a collar, but the club is quite happy for you to play in flip-flops. Many of the Nigerian members – about 90 percent of the total membership – take up the option.

Still more intriguing are those two huge bomb-crater bunkers that create the course's only topography. The one on the seventh is so huge it straddles the entire fairway. The bottom of this terrible pit is overgrown and riddled with snakes, and the many expatriates who play the course tend to reach into their pockets for a new ball rather than venture down. Not so concerned are the local youngsters, who are happy to search for balls to sell.

Snakes are not the course's only wildlife, as photographer

Paul Severn discovered to his cost. "There was a tiny ant on my hand, no bigger than the type you see in Britain all the time. I didn't think anything of it, but unfortunately they are poisonous. One bit me and it felt as painful as a wasp sting."

There is one exception to the crude course condition and it comes when you reach the browns. Inconsistent they may be, but each one has a brown-tender whose job it is to rake them smooth. Each brown-tender is a perfectionist, raking the entire surface impossibly flat after each group has putted out. He will even rake out the minuscule indentations made by another rolling ball if he feels it impedes your line to the hole.

The Air Assault course may be rough and ready, but despite all the hardships it still offers a fun and fascinating golfing experience – and the club's vibrant membership is testimony to that. Roy Donaldson takes his place among an army of keen golfers, ex-pats and locals, who enjoy their rounds day in, day out. For the most part, the course is packed. "It may not be Augusta," concludes Donaldson, "but the challenge of fading a ball round the corner of the dogleg, or getting up and down from thirty yards? That's exactly the same at both venues."

Places like the Air Assault Golf Club make us realize how many different golfing experiences the world has to offer. Most of us would love to give up everything, grab the clubs and go off playing golf around the world. Unfortunately, things like money, jobs and families make the idea little more than a pipe dream.

Unless, that is, your name is David Wood. For that's exactly what the fifty-year-old Californian did. In the summer of 2003 the bachelor decided he was bored of his job putting together corporate training videos. Golf was his passion, and he decided to indulge it.

"There wasn't anything holding me back," he recalls. "So I sold where I lived, which made enough to fund the trip, and put my stuff in storage. I turned the corporate-video business over to my partner. In the end it was an easy decision to make."

So on September 12, 2003 Wood packed a golf bag with ten clubs and a few clothes and set off on a journey that would see him play eighty rounds of golf in twenty-six countries on six continents – at a cost of $60,000. "It seemed to make sense to me to treat the adventure like a climb, starting at the bottom and working my way north," he says. "So I flew to Argentina to play Ushuaia, the world's southernmost course. My last round would be at the world's northernmost course in Norway. I had to get there before the end of the following summer, which in fact gave me about a year.

"So I started in the south and worked my way west around the world, following the sun and seeing where it took me."

But the golf trip from heaven got off to a hellish start. Wood found Ushuaia GC under snow, but elected to play it anyway. Then, driving across the Altiplano in an old bus on a dirt road from Salta, Argentina, to Saint Pedro de Atacama in Chile – at 15,000 feet – he suffered severe altitude sickness. He got it again at La Paz, Bolivia, en route to playing the world's highest course. "I guess you could say it was an inauspicious start," he admits.

Although he had a rough idea of which countries he would visit, Wood left the courses up to chance. "I would simply arrive at the next destination, jump on the Internet and find an interesting-looking place to play. I didn't exactly set out to play extreme courses, though I ended up playing a bunch. I was more interested in seeing golfers from other cultures. One thing that really hit home was that round the world, golfers really obey the rules. Everywhere I went the game was played formally, and with simple honesty. I really love that part of golf.

I found it everywhere."

Wood was also amazed to find an unofficial but nonetheless efficient global network of golfers. "When I told people what I was doing they got behind it. They would invite me into their homes and cook dinner for me and tell me to call a person at my next port of call. For example a gentleman in Perth, Australia, told me to call a guy in Singapore, who told me to call some fellow in Thailand . . . and he sent me to his contacts in Mission Hills, China, and then Spring City. It was phenomenal, and very friendly."

Wood's favorite destinations were Spring City and also New Zealand, a country he describes as "golfer's heaven." But amid the golf there were hardships. David fell badly ill five times, including food poisoning in India and Egypt. He became stuck in uprisings in Nepal and arrived in Bolivia shortly after 75 people had been killed in a riot.

"Maybe the worst part of all was getting kicked off a train in the Ukraine because I didn't have the right visa. They chucked me off at two a.m. and gave me an armed guard, which eventually put me on a train to Budapest, Hungary."

There were also times of intense loneliness. But despite those Wood never had a moment's doubt about what he was doing. He had long since decided to write the book of his journey, entitled *Around the World in 80 Rounds*. And when he finished the journey, making a streaky par on the last hole at Tromso in Norway at midnight in midsummer, he felt a great sense of accomplishment.

"I'm just a golf lover," he argues. "It's always been golf first, everything else second. The first thing I always pack are my golf clubs. I've always loved the thrill of discovering a great new course. To the detriment of my various careers, I play golf.

"I'm also a lover of public-course golf. I hate what golf has become where it's just a rich person's sport. I dislike the exclusivity part of it. I love the Scottish, democratic way, and I went looking for that. I wanted to find out if there were other golf fans like me around the world who felt the same. Happily, there are. Lots."

David Wood's decision to drop everything and take off round the world playing golf is our final journey to the edge of golf. His desire to rediscover golf as an Everyman's game is a theme that has cropped up many times in these pages. Many have journeyed to the edge of golf because of what remains at its center.

Recently I was standing on the platform at Spean Bridge railway station, western Scotland. Right next to the station is a picturesque nine-hole golf course, and as I had a little wait for the train, I decided to check it out. I wandered over to the clubhouse. It was little more than a shed, and an honesty box was there to collect my green fee. A chart was on the wall, telling me that a year's unlimited golf on the most beautiful course, surrounded by a pine forest and in the shadow of Ben Nevis, would cost me $190.00.

The place made me think. There are three golf clubs near my house with the most palatial clubhouses but with flat, sterile, featureless courses. The make-up of these clubs suggests they were built to champion the social status of being a member of a golf club, rather than to champion the game itself. The experience of visiting them is one of finicky rules and dress codes, reserved parking spaces and clubhouse no-go areas, all smothered under a suffocating blanket of etiquette. They may boast USGA-spec greens and have a sharp green fee to match; two rounds would eat up my year's golf at Spean Bridge. The places appear to be set up to stifle genuine golfing passion. Despite being a mad-keen golfer, I have never once given a second thought to joining any of them.

Spean Bridge Golf Club is the opposite. Here is a place where the golf course comes first and the clubhouse – and its social trappings – a very distant second. As such it attracts people who quite simply love to play the game; here is a place where genuine passion can thrive. There is more inspiration to be had on Spean Bridge's first hole than on those other courses" entire eighteens – and Spean Bridge opens with a short par-3. It is the sort of club of which David Wood – and many of the golfers in this book – would approve. Traditional, mainstream club golf remains dominated by social convention, and to its cost. Of course the social, communal side is an important adjunct of golf; but as long as it takes precedence over the game itself, golf culture will marginalize the people who have the most fire for the game.

Others, however, have journeyed to the game's outer limits quite simply because they can. The characters in this book reveal golf's greatest quality as its versatility: what other game can you play on snow, on mountains, through streets, in a crypt, among wild beasts or even in a prison cell? What other game can you play wrapped up in five layers of clothes, or buck-naked? What other game lets you find out about yourself and your surroundings simultaneously? What other game improves spiritual as well as physical health, while allowing you to see new sights and meet new people?

The game of golf is uniquely multifaceted. It offers all of us the opportunity to explore new paths in the game, and yet so very few of us do. I am the perfect example. When I started researching this book, my relationship with golf was based purely on my ability to play it. Good play was satisfying; but bad play, and there was a lot more of that, could make me quite depressed.

In short, I had forgotten how to enjoy the game. A look across the course at my fellow sportsmen suggested to me that I was not alone; the stock golfing countenance appeared to be a kind of resigned, stoical grimace. Smiles were at a premium, laughter approaching mythical status. For the score-obsessed amateur wretch, a round of golf has all the joy and enchantment of a migraine.

An interview with Kim Kelly at Australia's Coober Pedy pulled me up. Here was a man playing his golf in a landscape he described to me as "the arse-end of the world," on a featureless, flat, roasting-hot course – yet I found his ability to revel in the whole experience uplifting. Kelly's golfing experience did not revolve around making birdies and avoiding bogeys; it was about getting out there and socking a ball around. With that as your criterion for pleasure, you'll never have another bad day on a golf course.

One after the other, the stars of this book showed me how to enjoy golf again. Long-distance players Andre Tolme and David Ewen showed me how to use golf as a medium to appreciate your surroundings; the clothes-free golfers of New Zealand revealed graphically how it is possible to compete without being hung up on your score; and power hitter Sean Fister reminded me of the plain, potent pleasure of smashing the guts out of the ball.

Naturally I still enjoy a good tussle with the scorecard, but I can now see that as part of golf, and not the be-all and end-all. My emotions no longer go up and down with my score, and this improved perspective has of course helped my game. But the best part – and for this I am truly grateful to every golfer in this book – is my rediscovered appetite for playing. The first tee is no longer a place of impending doom, but the launching point for another unique adventure.

Appendix 1: Miscellany

Tips for speed golf

Thanks to Xtreme golfers Bob Babbitt and Tom Huddle.

- Select a putter, wedge and 7-iron. It's hard to control anything longer on the move.
- Get a small bag. You play early, almost in the dark for the first hole or two, so the grass is dewy and the grips get wet.
- Warm up. If you're not going to do that, take the first two or three holes easy.
- Slow down on the greens. In your final score a stroke represents a minute, so take your time and keep your score down. The biggest mistake is rushing your putts; you end up hockey-pucking it around and you don't want to do that.
- Forget the practice swing. Just hit the ball. It'll take time to get used to that, but this will change you mentally for your normal golf.

Antarctica rules

Scott Base "golf club" has fifteen rules for those heading out on to the ice:

1. 12-inch clean and place.
2. One club-length's drop from petrified seal droppings.
3. Melt pools are considered water hazards. Drop clear with a one-shot penalty.
4. Balls lost down seal or fish holes are out-of-bounds.
5. Interference with your ball by skua – replace ball, no penalty. But if it flies off with it, one-shot penalty.
6. Cover divots if over one mukluk (snowshoe) deep.
7. The ball will be considered holed if within one body length from the ball – heel to ball, head to pin.
8. Pressure ridges and cracks are out of bounds.
9. Orcas, penguins and seals have right of way.
10. Birdies can be claimed if you hit a skua.
11. If you are caught cheating, you must shout in the clubhouse, or at the completion of your game. Everyone would then know the shouting person had cheated.
12. You are not permitted to handle, remove, clean or replace other players' balls. However, you may kiss them prior to the game if you so desire.
13. The use of artificial stimulants during play, while not compulsory, is strongly recommended.
14. A knowledge of the rules of the Royal and Ancient Golf Club of St. Andrews is permitted; however, anyone caught applying them will be disqualified.
15. You must enjoy yourself completely.

Walter Langstaff's actual patent application for the bulls-pizzle golf ball – July 1912

This invention relates to golf and other balls of the kind made up on a core and has for its object to manufacture such balls with a core of a resilient animal substance which at present is more or less a waste product of the slaughterhouse; hence the cores are very low in first cost, and although very cheap to produce the balls possess all the requisite resiliency.

According to this invention I make the core of the ball from a piece of the pizzle of a bull or bullock, or where this is not sufficiently large in cross section, I use two or more of such pieces and unite them together by pressure, by an adhesive and ordinary knitting or darning wool, or by any other suitable means.

In preparing the pizzle for ball cores, I proceed as follows: I first entirely remove every particle of skin leaving only the muscular and other fibers and tissue. I then hang the skinless organ to dry in a cool place until all the moisture has exuded or evaporated therefrom. Under ordinary atmospheric conditions in this country this would take about one month if the organ be suspended in a barn or shed so that the air can obtain free access to every part of it. When the moisture-free condition has been reached, which is ascertained by the feel and appearance of the dryness, the pieces desired for the ball cores may be cut off and worked to shape with suitable tools.

The ball is made up on this resilient animal substance core and ordinary knitting or darning wool and is finished in the ordinary way.

Cross-country golf – a history of ramblers and gamblers

In the P G Wodehouse tale "The Long Hole," published in 1922, two bounders play a cross-country golf match for the hand of one Miss Amanda Trivett. Needless to say, by the time they get back she is engaged to someone else.

While there are no real-life stories of golfers playing to win the girl, Wodehouse was not being too fanciful. In his day, crazy cross-country golf challenges were often set up as the basis for a flutter.

In 1830 the St. Andrews Gold Medal champion, Major William Holcroft, bet ten sovereigns that he could drive from the first tee at St. Andrews to the toll bar at Cupar, nine miles distant, in 200 teed shots. He did it easily.

In 1898 Freddie Tait backed himself to play the three miles from Royal St George's clubhouse, Sandwich, to the Cinque Ports Club, Deal in 40 teed shots. He was to hole out by hitting any part of the Deal clubhouse. Again, the bet was won convincingly, Tait lacing his 32nd shot through a window.

And in 1920 local folk bet against D Rupert Phillips and W Raymond Thomas that they could not play from the first tee of the Radyr Golf Club to the last hole at Southerndown – a distance of 20 miles – in under 1,200 shots. The wager was struck in the knowledge that the intervening land consisted of swamps, woods and ploughed sludge. But, armed with Ordnance Survey maps, the men struck a clever route that saw them hole out two days and 608 strokes later to scoop the loot.

Golf's biggest hitters

408 yards – Englishman Karl Hooper's 1999 blow is in the *Guinness Book of Records* for the longest carry under 1000m altitude.

515 yards – Mike Austin's amazing hit is one of many claims for the longest drive ever hit.

720 yards – Crunched by Paul Slater in 2005 on an airstrip at London City Airport.

787 yards – Pro Carl Hooper achieved this shot in the 1992 Texas Open – a shot that twanged off a cart path and shot off down a hill. Carl needed a 4-iron to get back to the fairway.

2,640 yards – Norwegian meteorologist Nils Lied decided the least resistance to a golf ball would be offered by pack ice, so in 1962 he struck out for Mawson Base, Antarctica. His drive – like hitting across San Francisco's Golden Gate Bridge and back again – suggested he was right.

6 miles – An American named Bill Ice found something even better than his namesake – gravity. Bill sailed out into the North Pacific and positioned his boat over the Mariana Trench, the world's deepest section of ocean. In firing a shot over the side he laid claim to an unverifiable six-mile drive – straight down.

40 miles – Hit by an unknown golfer at John O'Gaunt GC, Bedfordshire, England. The golfer's shot sliced into the back of a pick-up truck taking vegetables to London. The truck was traced to Covent Garden market, where the ball was found plugged in a pile of cabbages.

One million miles – Russian cosmonaut Mikhail Tyurin's space shot, struck in November 2006, would apparently have flown this far (according to NASA) during its estimated four-day earth orbit.

282 yards – while nowhere near the distances recorded above, Christian Sterning holds the world record for the longest carry with one arm. In 2006 he whacked a ball 282 yards with his left arm only.

Tips for mountain golf

Mountain golfer Ric Moore is also a club pro. Here are his two keys to slope success:

You must align your shoulders to the slope of the hill. It will help you make solid contact, and that's the most crucial thing – thin or heavy shots bring the most penalties.

Hit within yourself; if you stretch your swing you will lose balance.

Why eighteen?

Long-distance golfers Andre Tolme and David Ewen both saw fit to divide their cross-country journeys into eighteen holes. But why is a round of golf eighteen holes long?

The traditional explanation of this apparently arbitrary figure runs something like this: St. Andrews' original layout was a linear twelve holes, of which ten were played twice – a round of twenty-two holes. Then in 1764 the first four holes were made into two longer ones, making ten holes, eight of which were played twice – a round of eighteen holes. By 1858 the number had been fortified by the cutting of an extra hole on each twice-played green.

And the number caught on, although it was not until 1950 that eighteen holes became the stipulated layout for a round of golf.

For some reason, this answer satisfies people; no one presses on to question where that original number of twelve came from.

Lyrics to "I'm Going Golfing Tomorrow"

The last song of *Golf: the Musical*

MAN 1:
The north wind is blowing,
It's ten below and snowing,
But I'm going golfing tomorrow.
We're getting a tsunami,
My caddy wants his mommy,
But I'm going golfing tomorrow.
Let hail fall from the sky, let avalanches roar,
Hey, that's what I carry those three wedges for,
Sure the weather stinks,
But I'll be on the links,
'Cause I'm going golfing tomorrow.

MAN 2:
My wife has a fever,
I really hate to leave her,
But I'm going golfing tomorrow.
A man must have his leisure,
And though she may have a seizure,
I'm going golfing tomorrow.
I won't be by her side, but I guess it's just as well
'Cause she'll be in a coma at Beth Israel,
She's under quarantine, and so I will be seen,
Out on the green tomorrow.

WOMAN:
Oy vey! My son's bar mitzvah starts at half-past two,
He's waiting at the temple, mind if I play through?

MAN 3 (an elderly man):
My days now are numbered,
My movements are encumbered,
But I'm going golfing tomorrow.
Soon they will inter me,
But that won't deter me,
'Cause I'm going golfing tomorrow.
Yes, soon my soul will pass, that's just the way it goes,
But I'll keep golfing as I decompose,
(hacks up a hairball and putts it toward stage left)
And in my grave behind the steeple,
I'll dig up three more people,
And we'll go golfing tomorrow.

ALL:
There's not much that's weirder, than golfers in a theater,
But you'll go golfing tomorrow.
But we are also duffers, and each of us suffers,
'Cause we're not golfing tomorrow.
We'll be here on the stage, that's how we live our lives.
But we know that most of you were dragged here by your wives!
So, don't stay around for us,
Go play around for us,
When you go golfing tomorrow.

City rules

From the Shoreditch Urban Open Rulebook:

Spectators
No shouting "Get in the hole." It's an inanimate object and we're not American.

Equipment
Clubs: Authentic clubs only. No sharing of clubs.
Mat: Playing mats will be supplied by our kind carpet-manufacturing sponsor.
Ball: Balls will be supplied. These are not normal golf balls. We will be introducing the Mk IV.

Dress
Hats: Hats can be worn on the course. Novelty hats will be confiscated.
Shirts: Shirts must be of the tailored type with collars only. They must be tucked in.
Trousers: Smart tailored trousers to be worn, no jeans or denims. Plus fours will be laughed at.
Shoes: Proper golf shoes should not be worn, unless you plan on going clubbing afterwards.

290 over par

Andre Tolme's Golf Mongolia scorecard:

Hole 1
Distance: 144,607 yards (82.2 miles, 132.2km)
Par: 711
Shots: 833
Lost balls: 40
Days: 8

Hole 2
Distance: 83,242 yards (47.3 miles, 76.1km)
Par: 403
Shots: 430
Lost balls: 23
Days: 4

Hole 3
Distance: 62,240 yards (35.4 miles, 56.9km)
Par: 694
Shots: 344
Lost balls: 18
Days: 3

Hole 4
Distance: 117,370 yards (66.7 miles, 107.3km)
Par: 493
Shots: 631
Lost balls: 34
Days: 5.5

Hole 5
Distance: 139,794 yards (79.4 miles, 127.8km)
Par: 901
Shots: 771
Lost balls: 43
Days: 5.5

Hole 6
Distance: 78,210 yards (44.4 miles, 71.5km)
Par: 683
Shots: 436
Lost balls: 28
Days: 3

Hole 7
Distance: 112,447 yards (63.9 miles, 102.8km)
Par: 711
Shots: 609
Lost balls: 35
Days: 5

Hole 8
Distance: 151,935 (86.3 miles, 138.9km)
Par: 638
Shots: 893
Lost balls: 72
Days: 6

Hole 9
Distance: 153,686 yards (86.3 miles, 140.5km)
Par: 839
Shots: 907
Lost balls: 59
Days: 6
Hole 10
Distance: 147,122 yards (83.6 miles, 134.5km)
Par: 699
Shots: 891
Lost balls: 22
Days: 7

Hole 11
Distance: 72,631 yards (41.3 miles, 66.4km)
Par: 414
Shots: 387
Lost balls: 21
Days: 3

Hole 12
Distance: 140,669 yards (79.9 miles, 128.6km)
Par: 565
Shots: 748
Lost balls: 17
Days: 5

Hole 13
Distance: 196,783 yards (111.8 miles, 179.9km)
Par: 845
Shots: 1096
Lost balls: 20
Days: 7

Hole 14
Distance: 97,899 yards (55.6 miles, 89.5km)
Par: 772
Shots: 527
Lost balls: 9
Days: 4

Hole 15
Distance: 132,574 yards (75.3 miles, 121.2km)
Par: 621
Shots: 778
Lost balls: 21
Days: 5

Hole 16
Distance: 113,213 yards (64.3 miles, 103.5km)
Par: 677
Shots: 627
Lost balls: 10
Days: 4

Hole 17
Distance: 136,075 yards (77.3 miles, 124.4km)
Par: 706
Shots: 756
Lost balls: 26
Days: 5

Hole 18
Distance: 91,008 yards (51.7 miles, 83.2km)
Par: 508
Shots: 506
Lost balls: 11
Days: 4

Totals
Distance: 2,171,505 yards (1,233.8 miles, 1,985.2km)
Par: 11,880
Shots: 12,170
Lost balls: 509
Days: 90

Golf's speed merchants

18 holes (individual) – Gary Wright (Australia), 28 minutes 9 seconds (fellow Australian Rick Baker managed 26 minutes 20 seconds but he was allowed to hit the ball before it came to rest)

18 holes (fourball) – Michael Armitt, John Calcutt, Tom Greaves and Gordon Archibald in 73 minutes 49 seconds

18 holes (team) – 8 minutes 46 seconds, set in 2006 by a team of 25 caddies from Kiawah Island, South Carolina

Fastest hole (minimum 500 yards) – Phil Naylor (England), 1 minute 52 seconds

In 1992 Mark Calcavecchia and John Daly were both fined by the U.S. Tour for playing too *quickly*. They completed the final round in the Tournament Players' Championship in two hours and three minutes. Daly fired an 80 and Calcavecchia an 81.

Tundra golf – how to deal with hazards

Courtesy of *Golf on the Tundra* – the ultimate set of winter rules

A. Sledders in the fairway

If a player's ball is interfered with by the head or body of a sledder, the player is allowed a drop where the ball would have landed or a free shot from the ball's original position.

B. Cross-country skiers/tracks

Should a skier interfere with a player's backswing, the player is allowed to hit again without penalty. Cross-country ski and snowmobile tracks may be treated as you treat cart paths during the summer – free swing and stance relief.

C. Freezing on the green

This hazard is common among players who take too much time lining up their putts and is another good reason to avoid slow play, and can sometimes result in a penalty.

D. Snowmobiles

While their tracks provide a great lie, snowmobiles themselves pose a great danger, as many drivers may not even see you as they scout the horizon for cross-country skiers to run over.

E. Irate greenskeepers

Unenlightened greenskeepers may not recognize the assets of Tundra Golf, under the misconception that play during winter months may damage a course. The truth is, the frozen ground actually protects turf from divotting. However, should an angry groundsperson disrupt your round, play may be continued at a later date from the last hole finished with no penalty to any players.

Appendix 2: Contacts

Golf courses

Colonsay GC
Isle of Colonsay, Scotland PA61 7YP
Email: golf@machrin.free-online.co.uk
Phone: 01951 200364

Club de Golf Rio Lluta
Pampa de los vientos, cerro sombrero, Km 7,
Arica, Tarapaca, Chile
Email: calvarez@cormetar.cl
Phone: 0056 582 23377

Lomas Santa Fe Executive Golf Course
1580 Sun Valley Road, Solana Beach, CA 92075
Phone: 001 858 755 0195

Opal Fields Coober Pedy Golf Club
Lot 1509 Rowe Dve, Coober Pedy, South Australia, 5723
Phone: 0061 886 725 353

Air Assault Golf Club
WAN-6206 Port Harcourt, Rivers, Nigeria
Phone: 00234 8423 2527

Skukuza Golf Club
Kruger National Park, South Africa
Website: www.thegolfclub.co.za/skukuza.htm
Email: info@thegolfclub.co.za
Phone: 0027 217 120 980

Furnace Creek Resort
Highway 190, Death Valley, California 92328, USA
Website: www.furnacecreekresort.com
Email: info-fc@xanterra.com
Phone: 001 760 786 2345

Competitions

Shoreditch Urban Open
Email: the_committee@sgcgolf.com
Website: sgcgolf.com

UX Open
UXGA Tour Properties, LLC, 103 Matilda Place, Fairfield, CT 06824
Website: www.uxopen.com
Email: dkelly@uxopen.com
Phone: 001 203 255 2891

MacKenzie Muster festival (nude golf)
Website: www.naturist.co.nz/muster.htm
Email: naturally@xtra.co.nz

Pillar Mountain Golf Classic
Pillar Mountain Golf, PO Box 1906, Kodiak, AK 99615
Email: wkoning@ptialaska.net
Phone: 001 907 486 9489

Remax world long-drive championships
Long Drivers of America, Ltd., 600 Henrietta Creek Drive Suite 200,
Roanoke, TX 76262
Website: www.longdrivers.com
Email: sellinger@longdrivers.com
Phone: 001 888 233 4654

Speed golf competitions
Speedgolf International, PMB 140, 333 W. North Avenue, Chicago,
Illinois 60610
Website: www.speedgolfinternational.com
Email: tscott@speedgolfinternational.com

Trashmasters
PO Box 6200, Snowmass Village, Colorado
Website: www.trashmasters.com
Email: contact@trashmasters.com
Phone 001 970 927-TRASH

Other contacts

Natural Born Golfers
Website: www.naturalborngolfers.com
Email: headquarter@naturalborngolfers.com
Phone: 0049 4085 389 981

Ahlgrim and Sons Funeral Home

201 N. Northwest Hwy, Palatine, Illinois
Phone: 001 847 358 7411

Golf Mongolia
Website: www.golfmongolia.com
Email: andre@golfmongolia.com

Books to read

The Tip of the Iceberg – Yarns and Ditties of New Zealanders in Antarctica
David L Harrowfield
South Latitude Research

Par 10,000 – A Golfing Odyssey across Mountains, Moorlands and Fields
David Ewen
Mainstream Publishing

Commitment to Honor – A Prisoner of War Remembers Vietnam
Colonel George R Hall and Pat Hall

Golf on the Tundra
The official rulebook of the Tundra Golf Association
The Frozen Foursome
X Communications